The Fully Lived Life

Rescuing Our Souls from All that Holds Us Back

by Dr. Merry C. Lin

THE
Life fULLY LIVED

RESCUING Our SOULS from ALL that Holds Us BACK

"I have come that they may have life, and have it to the full." (John 10:10)

Dr. Merry C. Lin
Clinical Psychologist

CASTLE QUAY BOOKS
WWW.CASTLEQUAYBOOKS.COM

The Fully Lived Life: Rescuing Our Souls from All that Holds Us Back

Copyright ©2014 Dr. Merry C. Lin
All rights reserved
Printed in Canada
International Standard Book Number: 978-1-927355-50-3
ISBN 978-1-927355-51-0 EPUB

Published by:
Castle Quay Books
Pickering, Ontario, L1W 1A5
Tel: (416) 573-3249
E-mail: info@castlequaybooks.com   www.castlequaybooks.com

Edited by Marina Hofman Willard
Cover design by Burst Impressions
Printed at Essence Publishing, Belleville, Ontario

Library and Archives Canada Cataloguing in Publication

Lin, Merry C. L., author
        The fully lived life : rescuing our souls from all that holds
us back / Merry C. Lin ; Marina Hofman Willard, editor.
Issued in print and electronic formats.
ISBN 978-1-927355-50-3 (pbk.)
        1. Self-actualization (Psychology)—Religious aspects—
Christianity. 2. Self-actualization (Psychology). I. Title.
BV4598.2.L55 2013   248   C2013-907948-3

Table of Contents

Introduction

"Are you tired? Worn out? Burned out on reli-
gion? Come to me. Get away with me and you'll
recover your life. I'll show you how to take a real
rest. Walk with me and work with me—watch
how I do it. Learn the unforced rhythms of grace.
I won't lay anything heavy or ill-fitting on you.
Keep company with me and you'll learn to live
freely and lightly."

Matthew 11:28–30, MSG

I had finally had enough.

I woke, and my body refused to get out of bed. After a restless night, I lay there, exhausted and overwhelmed. Head pounding, muscles aching. The sun peered through the blinds heralding the new day, but I wanted to yell at it, *Shut up!* It was mocking me.

That's when I knew I was losing it.

For 15 years I'd run a busy counselling practice and raised my kids. Every day, I woke to the drumbeat of *go, go, go* pounding in my head as I drove myself to keep going. No time to pause, no time to relax. You ever feel that way?

But I was finally crashing, beaten down by discouragement and a growing depression that squeezed out all rationality. I was an emotional mess; I hated my life and who I'd become. I wasn't sleeping, I had no energy and I was burned out. Just getting up each morning was like scaling a mountain, and I was no longer finding any joy in anything I did. Spiritually, I'd become as dry as an abandoned well. I'd lost the will to pray long ago, let alone the desire to read my Bible or attend church.

In this desert, I realized I was trapped, unable to break out of the prison my life had become. I was slowly dying, surrounded by constant demands for my time and drained by others' expectations.

No matter what I did, it was never enough.

Despite knowing I was called to be a hope-bearer for others in despair, I couldn't bear the burden of caring for them in my counselling office any longer. I couldn't hear their painful stories without losing another piece of myself. There was no way I could continue pretending to care as they sought healing from God in the midst of their suffering and personal crises. I was failing myself, my family, my team, my clients, my community and my God.

As bad as I felt then, it wasn't until a time of reflective prayer with two of my trusted friends that I finally broke down completely. I remember the moment as clearly as when it happened. It was the day my headlong tumble into depression and burnout began.

It's been three years since then as I write this, but I can still feel the hard floor on my knees as I hunched sobbing, held tight by my friend. And I can still feel the comfort of my encounter with Jesus that day.

It was during *lectio divina,* as we reflected on the passage in John 5:1–9. Jesus encountered a lame man lying by the pool of Bethesda, waiting 38 years to be healed. This pool of water was purported to have healing qualities when the water was stirred, but the lame man told Jesus he had no one to help him. Others were always jumping in ahead of him.

We imagined ourselves in the scene as the passage was read aloud. I tried to imagine myself lying lame by the pool, but it didn't feel right. So I envisioned myself getting up and helping others into the pool. I knew I was crippled, but I hid it secretly, desperately hurting on the inside as I focused on my task of assisting others in need.

Then Jesus approached me, unspeakable compassion on his face, and asked what I wanted.

In an instant, I fell forward onto my knees and cried out, *"When is it my turn?"*

I began to weep uncontrollably, surrounded by my loving friends who embraced me and cried with me. So deep was my sorrow, I could not stop crying.

Beyond my exhaustion and emotional fatigue, I was crying for the years I had secretly felt abandoned by God, forgotten by others and valued only for what I could do or give to them. I was seen only in the light of how well I was able to meet their demands and needs. I had become an empty shell, and there was a wide chasm between me and my true identity as a child of God. My sense of worth was dictated by the approval of others, to the point that I'd lost all sight of myself and what my life had become.

Looking back, it wasn't until the Lord took me to the end of myself that I finally had no choice but to let go. Exhausted and hopelessly discouraged, I crashed. But this was a gift, too, because me being so deep in the crippling darkness of depression meant that he could take me on the incredible journey of facing the emptiness within my heart and soul.

And finding him *there* with me in my desert has literally changed my life.

Wherever you are in life right now, I'm sure there have been many unexpected turns along the way. You aren't where you thought you'd be, whatever you first dreamt your life would be—the fairy-tale marriage and family, a highly successful career, a passion for God reaping you the blessings of faithful service. Instead, the realities of your life may be keeping you stuck, unable to break free no matter how hard you pray. I know what it's like to feel completely overwhelmed by life's demands, weary beyond belief and wondering where all your hope has gone.

You may know you're blessed, that you really have a "good life" and are very fortunate, but you may still have lost your joy in it. You go through dreary daily routines, fulfilling your duties to your family, work and God, but your heart is dry. Where is the passion and joy within the unending grey monotony of life? This "good life" you have steals your right to complain, so you "suck it up" and keep trudging along.

We all try to ignore the emptiness of the soul. But the Bible says, "*Deep calls to deep*" (Psalm 42:7). There is something *inescapable* within each of our souls that hungers so painfully that we can't even begin to put it into words, something so deep it won't go away no matter how hard we try. As David said, "*As the deer* **pants** *for streams of water, so my soul* **pants** *for you, my God. My soul* **thirsts** *for God, for the living God*" (Psalm 42:1–2, emphasis mine).

We aren't meant to live a dead life. A superficial life. A life oblivious to the stirrings of our hearts. It is only in that mysterious depth of our souls that we sense there's something missing that's core to life; it's a painful awareness that we must finally acknowledge and reach into and find God.

God wants you to meet him in this deep place, in the inner recesses of your heart, to meet him there *face to face*, so he can change your life. He wants to bring you back to life, to know you intimately so that you may know yourself in his love, as he first created you to be. He wants to free you and take over fully because he knows best how you were created to live—completely surrendered to him.

For then he knows you will experience the extraordinary in your life, the *full life* that is his perfect will for you. A life lived *fully*.

And so, as you begin, I urge you to slow down. Don't whip through this book like an anxious teenager looking for the next thrill, and the next, and the next. *This* is the finish line, the place where you accept God's love and sovereign will over all he's brought to your life. There's not one more thing to check off on your "to-do" list today. Slow down and hear what the Lord wants to say to you here.

In our culture we're living in a pandemic of ignored introspection. Action is valued over reflection, and all too often we rush through life mindlessly, always on to the next thing. And so we don't seem to grow through our hardships, or we find ourselves stuck and don't know why. Such lack of reflectiveness is a formula for a human shipwreck.

Have you been that shipwreck?

Have you ever taken time to get to know the longing inside? Often people are so busy simply surviving life they forget that really *living* requires some downtime

1 = "Not at all true."
2 = "Sometimes."
3 = "Often."
4 = "Most of the time."
5 = "Completely true."

Question	Score
1. I am juggling many responsibilities and feel like I can't keep up with the demands in my life.	
2. When I stop, I feel physically or emotionally exhausted.	
3. I wish I could take a significant break to rest and reflect on my life with some soul-searching.	
4. My spiritual life feels dry and lifeless.	
5. I have a hard time sensing God's presence in my life or experiencing his love for me.	

Question	Score
6. I seem to struggle with the same issues over and over in my life and don't know why.	
7. I don't like to think about negative or uncomfortable things for too long, and I distract myself to feel better.	
8. I'm uncomfortable with strong emotions and would rather focus on practical, sensible things.	
9. I feel stuck, knowing I need to make some changes but unsure where to start.	
10. People rely on me and think of me as competent, but I don't know how I feel or even if I care anymore.	

reflecting on what they're actually *doing* with their lives. I'm guilty of that all too often. Take just a moment to consider this quick self-assessment.

If your total score is 10 to 20, you appear to have good self-awareness. Use this opportunity to learn how to truly live out what you know. Really allow yourself to absorb what the Lord says about living life to the full.

If your total score is between 21 and 30, your life could use some improvement. Take a look at the scores of 3 or higher to identify what you need to focus your attention on.

If your total score is between 31 and 50 take heed. You and people like you are living life in a less-than-full way God never intended. Seize this opportunity to recalibrate your life, and believe the promise that when you dig deep, as uncomfortable as it may be, the rewards are sure to follow.

Regardless of where you are, slow down *and let yourself be rescued.* As you read, when something catches your attention, *stop* and ponder it. Turn it over in your mind, apply it to different circumstances and situations of your life. How might that have changed what happened back there? When something here connects, stop and ask, "What am I feeling?" "What does this mean for me?" "What are you telling me, God?"

Go deep. And allow yourself to process and reflect. Journal your thoughts and capture your journey. Take a year or longer to read this book if necessary. In a time-starved life, it's always the case that we forfeit introspection. If you're like most people, you've scorned the value of allowing yourself to sit quietly and reflect on something that's personal, *just for you.* The competing demands of a multitude of tasks before us would keep you shipwrecked. But fortunately, you haven't lost your God-given ability to grow and to change from the inside out.

Slow down.

While you could certainly use this book as another prescription to treat your symptoms, stop right now and ask if God wants *more* for you than short-term solutions-oriented therapy. Focusing only on stopping the pain will prevent you from finding solutions that will actually address your deeper problem. Quick fixes can be valuable and provide you with good, concrete advice, but that's not this book.

Like long-term insight-oriented therapy, this book is meant to guide you on a self-reflective journey to help you make deep personal change for *life.* At the end of each chapter, you will find reflection questions to help you go deeper, in the section entitled "Digging Deep." These exercises are offered for you as guidelines, not prescriptions, so don't let yourself be overwhelmed by the tasks. Do as much or as little as you choose. Go back as many times as you need to. You pace it. Listen to God's leading on what you choose to do or not do, as well as the timing.

Spend time journaling your answers to the reflection questions. Do all of your journaling in the same notebook or computer folder so you can track your progress as you finish each chapter—and check back in a year or two to see how far you've come.

If you do this, let yourself go deep into the unexplored "scary" places, those vulnerable areas. If you allow yourself to get honest and face your true emotions, you will begin to grieve what you've been missing. You already know it will be painful, but I promise you, it will carry with the pain a joy you've never known before. Your Father—the one who loves you exactly the way you are and sees you perfectly— waits for you. And I promise you that meeting him there will be life-changing.

Whatever led you to pick up this book, the title or description, a recommendation or "chance," *God* led you to it. Pursue that leading. Jesus said, "*A man can receive nothing unless it has been given him from heaven*" (John 3:27, NASB). I pray that somehow the longing in your soul for more, the hunger deep within you for something unnameable, the part of you that cries "Is this it?" as you contemplate your life, will lead you to search for a full life with your Father—a fully lived life.

Don't ignore the call to freedom. Stop pretending. Your life depends on it.

I invite you now to open your heart to the possibility of more. Begin your journey of introspection and freedom. Seek out the life of fullness Jesus promises you. Section 1 will lay out the ways you are soul weary and the barriers that prevent you from living a full life. Section 2 will draw you closer to God's heart for you as you choose to return to the full life he offers. And Section 3 describes the life of fullness you are meant to live—a fully lived life.

Over the years, I've walked with many clients in this same way, and when they've had the courage to "go deep," I've had the privilege of seeing our Father heal their brokenness and pain, bring astonishing beauty out of ashes and miraculously transform their lives. And so it's my joy to dedicate this book to these courageous people of faith. They have been an awe-inspiring testimony to me as I've watched them choose to live *the full life*. You will hear their stories (their identity and certain details have been changed to preserve their anonymity) and be inspired along your way.

If you will slow down to take this journey now, you *will* be transformed.

That's not my promise; it's God's. And it's my sincere prayer for you as you read this book.

Come and see. Our Father is inviting you to a full life with him.

SECTION I

Soul Weary

That is why many among you are weak and sick,
and a number of you have fallen asleep.

1 Corinthians 11:30

CHAPTER 1

Does God Care?

God, are you avoiding me? Where are you when
I need you?

Psalm 10:1, MSG

Yvette stared at me stonily, mouth compressed tightly. She had finally revealed the story of her tragic history, the years of abuse she had endured at the hands of her father, who used her sexually and robbed her of the ability to trust another man. My eyes filled with tears as I heard her story, but she remained stoic even in the face of my compassion. We looked at each other, I, mute in my sorrow for her, she, silent in her taut self-control. Finally, she spoke in a monotone, telling me she was "fine." Yet her anxiety was betrayed by the tightness in her expression and the stiff way she held her shoulders and clenched her fists. After another moment of silence, she changed subjects and began speaking about her problems with insomnia and unexplained aches and pains.

A faithful follower of Jesus Christ, Yvette came to see me when she began to suffer from depression and baffling panic attacks that would not lift, no matter how often she prayed or delved into God's promises through the Scriptures. At the time I first met her, she was serving on three different ministries and was lauded for her exemplary "servant's heart." But secretly, to her shame, she could not break free from her struggles with depression, and she was afraid that she was going to one day act out on her increasingly dark and suicidal thoughts. And so she fought her shame with anger and self-hatred, beating herself up for her failure as a Christian.

To be honest, Yvette was hard to like, at least at first. I don't think she liked *me*. There was a hardness to her, a bitterness that was hard to penetrate. I don't know why she continued to come faithfully, because I could not seem to make a dent in her guard. Every time I thought I was beginning to see some vulnerability in her eyes, she shut it down quickly. But no matter how often she blasted me away with her anger, I kept picturing her as that little girl, defenceless and scared. Who did she have to protect her? No wonder she had to put up a protective wall around her heart.

I also knew that because of the wounds she had suffered growing up, Yvette had a canyon between her head knowledge of God's love for her and her experience of that truth in her heart. She knew the "rules" of her faith, which she followed strictly, but she didn't know the heart of her Father. Not really. And I knew that because of this rift, she was missing out on the life of abundance—the full life—that was supposed to be her birthright as a Christ-follower.

The Legacy of Adam and Eve

From the Garden of Eden until today, we have all struggled with believing in God's love for us. We question whether God will really pull through for us; we wonder if he's holding out on us and what we might be missing out on; we doubt if God *really* knows our needs and if he will meet them; and we question the trustworthiness of God's promises as we wonder whether we need to take things into our own hands.

We all know the story. The serpent whispered into Eve's ear, "God's holding out on you. He doesn't want you to have the very thing you need." The moment she allowed his sly whispers to create doubt in her mind, she began to fear that she was missing out on something big. And we know how infectious fear can be, as Adam chose also to eat from the same fruit of doubt. And after they took that bite of the fruit, they began to feel shame and, out of that shame, a fear of being naked before God, and so they hid themselves. Fear and doubt began to control them and dictate to them what they should do, even forcing them to turn away from the only One who could free them and heal them. Imagine being forced to leave the Garden of Eden, the only home you've known, and begin life separated from your loving Father. Imagine the horror that must have gripped them as they faced a life without him to protect and guide them. That legacy continues to haunt us today.

How many times have you questioned God's goodness and love for you when something difficult happens? I don't know about you, but I never faced that reality until I was forced to look into the darkness in my heart. Like many people, I shielded myself with busyness and attempts to win God's love by my good works. And then once I was exhausted by my efforts, I blamed God for abandoning me. I wondered whether the abundant life was a lie. I looked around and saw pain and chaos in my life and in the world. And I broke down.

Where is this life of *fullness* we're supposed to have? Especially when your life doesn't look much better than those who don't even believe in God?

Can I Trust You, God?

One of the most painful truths I've ever had to face was that I wasn't living a life of fullness with God because *I did not trust him.* I couldn't. And I could not trust him because I didn't feel safe enough with him…I had never experienced him as trustworthy in my life.

Maybe you know what I'm talking about.

God has let us down; he hasn't acted in the way we think he should have. We're taught that God loves us, but when we see the pain and suffering we all experience, there's a disconnect we can't reconcile.

And if I can't reconcile that then I have *no choice* but to rely on myself to get through life. And I eat the fruit. I make my own way. I try to "earn" God's approval. But fear-based living only leads to legalism, and duty-based obedience is not a life lived fully.

I used to hear leaders talk about God's love and what it means to be his "beloved child," and my inner cynic stood back and scoffed. Do you tell a mother who's just lost her son to suicide that she needs to surrender more fully to God in faith? Or a husband whose wife has just left him for the third time for another woman that he should just "let go and let God" be in control?

What do you tell Yvette?

Do You Really Care About Me, God?

When you line up the pain and suffering of life with the words of God's love, we feel this disconnect deep in our hearts. That's when our heart splits off and God's Word becomes empty words. We're told we need to believe more and have more faith, but our experience of life tells us there's something different from what we're seeing in God's Word.

Brent Curtis and John Eldredge say it well in *The Sacred Romance:*

> In the secret places of our hearts, we believe God is the One who did not protect us from these things or even the One who perpetrated them on us. Our questions about him make us begin to live with a deep apprehension that clings anxiously to the depths of our hearts… Do you really care for me, God? This is the question that has shipwrecked many of our hearts, leaving them grounded on reefs of pain and doubt, no longer free

to accompany us on spiritual pilgrimage…What are we to make of God's wildness in allowing these things to happen?[1]

And so we cope by shutting down our hearts, buttoning down our passions tightly, and ignoring our emotional life to the point that we completely lose touch with our hearts. It's more comfortable living in our rational minds, isn't it? I know I find it easier not to feel sometimes. Less painful. And since our sin struggles are probably rooted in our wayward hearts anyway, it's safer to clamp down on our uncontrolled emotions. Sure, we squeeze the very life out of our souls and the joy out of our lives. But at least we're in control.

Some of us have operated so long at the intellectual level that we take pride in maintaining tight control of ourselves, in being able to step back from our emotions to focus on the task at hand or the problem to be solved, to just "get on with it" without all the fuss of the emotional baggage that some other people seem to have. Well-ordered efficiency is valued over the messiness of relationship. Connection *with* God is replaced by knowledge *of* God.

Programs and principles rule over our wayward hearts, directing us to colour neatly within the prescribed Christian lines. Life becomes a series of principles, and relationships become a list of "to-dos." The music of our inner life, the passion and sorrows of our hearts, the life of the deep places within us, all of this dies a slow death under the unrelenting tyranny of our intellect. We end up sleepwalking through our lives.

Does this sound like you at all? Do you want more but you're afraid to go deeper? Or are you ready to ask, "Is life working for me? Am I truly living the life I was meant to live?"

For Yvette, soul rescue meant opening her heart to the One who *is* heaven on earth. Connection *with* God instead of knowledge *of* God. After years of burying her battered heart, she finally begun to experience her Father's love for her. Slowly, after months of sitting with her, holding her pain for her, accepting her anger, loving her through her darkest moments, I had the privilege of seeing Yvette come awake.

It wasn't through my answers to her questions or the practical tips I could give her—for what answers can you give someone who has suffered the greatest of betrayals? Instead, it was through a sacred time each week in my little office when she was able to experience the tender love of her Father as she chose to dig deep and face her wounds and broken trust. Today, Yvette is an incredible encouragement to others because she reflects God's love while walking with them through the dark valleys of their lives.

Digging Deep

What about you? Are you longing for a transformation like Yvette's, rescue for *your* soul?

If your heart is buried, you may not feel it. But if you're curious or feel any stirring, this process of introspection and discovery could be revealing for you. As you read the chapters that follow, get gut-honest with yourself. The Lord is waiting to awaken your soul if you'll allow him to speak to your heart.

I can promise you, it will be worth it.

CHAPTER 2

Do I Trust God?

Doubled up with pain, I call to God all the day long. No answer. Nothing.

Psalm 22:2, MSG

George sat before me, tears slowly making their way down his leathery cheeks. His grief was palpable—not in what he said, but in how he fought to keep his emotions in check as he swallowed back his tears, unable to maintain eye contact for fear of losing control in the face of my compassion. But stemming the tide of his sorrow was an impossible task because a lifetime of pain was finally, painfully, coming to light.

Formerly gregarious and known for his positive attitude, George was deeply ashamed of his "failure" to maintain his confidence and stoic belief in the goodness of God. This seemingly faithful Christian man had spent a lifetime hiding from the truth of his hidden distrust of God. He had buried his hurt and feelings of abandonment to minister abroad as a missionary who had given his life to serve the Lord. Forty-two years later, George sat before me a broken man, having just lost his wife to cancer. Deep down, he believed God would come through for him when he prayed for healing for his wife, especially after he had given so much to serving the Lord.

How could his supposedly loving Father do this to him?

As George and I started to work through his grief, he began to uncover the devastating hurt he had experienced as a young boy when his missionary parents left him in a boarding school while working overseas. It was at this Christian boarding school that George experienced abuse and terror at the hands of the teachers. Today, he recalls many nights of crying himself to sleep, praying to God to save him and longing for his mom and dad to come and rescue him. But they never came.

The biggest blow of all when he was 11 years old: he received the news from his principal that his mother had died. He described receiving this news calmly, with a feeling of numbness. Looking back, he realized he had shut down his heart. He couldn't bear any more pain, and so he disengaged from his loneliness and fear.

And now, 42 years later, it was all coming back.

Heartbreak…loss…betrayal…why does God allow these dark and inexplicable valleys in our lives? Even as I write this, a very dear friend of mine has been taken to the end of herself with the recent death of two close family members, and this after struggling through a very difficult year of many challenges and dark times. Just as she was reeling from the loss of one beloved family member, the second loss came, the day after the first funeral. She tells me she can't even pray at this point, so weary is her soul…so empty is her heart. And as my heart breaks for her, I can only pray, listening and walking with her through her valley. Nothing I do can alleviate her pain and the reality of living in this ragged, broken world.

What has God allowed to affect and define your story? Where has God disappointed you with unanswered prayers? When has he "betrayed your trust" by allowing you to experience devastating pain and loss? The scars on our hearts are there, and many of us may have chosen to cope by erecting a wall so that we'd stop being disappointed yet again by God.

That was certainly my story.

I was raised in a loving, Christian home, so the idea of trusting and obeying God was part of my life as a child. I grew up knowing the stories in the Bible and having a childlike confidence in the love, protection and provision of my heavenly Father. But my happy world ended when I was eight. My older brother died.

Much remains blurred in my child's remembrance of that time, save for several crystal-clear snapshots that still grip me today: the day my brother was rushed to the hospital after complaining of a headache and falling to the ground, unconscious; the months of watching my parents go back and forth to the hospital, faces drawn with worry; and then, the pivotal day when I was called into the principal's office and told that my brother had "passed away." I looked blankly at him; what did "pass away" mean? Then, the axis of my world shifted, the room spinning dizzily when the principal explained to me that my brother had died. How could that be? He was supposed to get better, wasn't he? The principal had to be wrong. Where were my mommy and daddy? They would correct this man.

And then, seeing my brother, a complete stranger, emaciated and bony, dressed in a black suit I had never seen, lying in his coffin, hands crossed stiffly over his chest. And the overpowering smell of the flowers, the low buzz of the people talking, the stuffy heat of the room. And then leaning over his coffin when no one was watching, poking my brother's face, feeling how waxy and cold his skin was. Who was that? No, that was not my brother. To this day, I cannot view any pictures of his funeral (who takes pictures at funerals?) without feeling the nauseous, hollow feeling rush over me again.

I don't remember everything about that season of grief, but I do know that it was a devastating time in the life of my family. As the youngest, I didn't understand everything that was happening. I only remember my parents disappearing and me feeling very much alone. I know now that they were grieving but trying to stay strong and stoic for us. They said only that my brother was in heaven, and so I thought as Christians we were supposed to accept God's capricious ways and move on. Today I know differently, as I now understand with an adult's perspective the intense agony that my parents must have endured. They were simply trying to cope with unbearable loss in the best way they knew how, not only because of the death of my brother, the beloved son who was going to be a pastor, but because of the *way* he died. For I learned much later, to my intense shock, that he died because of a careless accident by a nurse, causing my brother to choke to death. *And this was God's will?* My family was torn apart because of a *mistake?*

The Stronghold of Fear

For children that young, often the predominant emotion when losing a loved one is a strong sense of fear, a nameless sense of dread. I didn't grieve the loss of my brother at that time. I didn't even cry, but that day I was handed over to the tyrannical stronghold of fear. I was already a timid child, and fear became my constant companion. My parents had no clue, so I was scolded and teased mercilessly for my nervous ways. Anything new or unexpected was greeted with dread. What if something bad happened? I saw danger all around me.

Fear had its fierce grip on me, darkly staining many of my childhood memories. One memory in particular stands out starkly: when I was nine years old, we went to visit my cousins, and at some point during the visit, I fell asleep. Rather than taking me home, my parents decided to leave me there overnight. I woke up disoriented in the middle of the night, lying alone in a strange hallway without any pillows or blankets. Terror immediately struck. Where was I? Where were my parents? Terrified, I began screaming and howling loudly, "Mommy!"

The door burst open, and my aunt came out, her face dark with fury. As I cowered, wailing, she began yelling at me to be quiet. "Mommy, come get me now; don't leave me here!" My aunt told me that my parents weren't coming for me, that I had to wait until the morning, and then she stomped back into her room. For the rest of the unbearably long night, I lay crying quietly, curled up in the hallway, shivering with the cold, terrified of my mean aunt coming out to yell at me. Looking back, it seems like such a harmless memory, yet for that little nine-year-old girl it was fraught with traumatic terror, which marked me.

As I grew up, I developed all sorts of compulsive behaviours to cope, until they overtook my life and controlled me. Fear became my master, a voracious tyrant that took over more and more of my life. It became so much a part of the background music of my life that I stopped recognizing the discordant noise. It was only when I reached a point of paralysis and bondage in my mid-20s that, with a lot of work and God's help, I triumphed over the grip of fear in my life. End of chapter, right?

The Forgotten Child

We often tell our clients in counselling that recovery is like peeling back the layers of an onion. It's only when we've dealt with one aspect of our brokenness that God brings another to the surface. And then another: one after another, deeper and deeper layers of our story knock at the doors of our heart, seeking to be heard and longing for healing.

Well, let me just say that I can preach it, but I have to admit that it was much harder to see that happening in my own life. Having worked hard to move on with my life, I gave no further thought to the loss of my brother as a child. After all, I was busy getting on with the stuff of life, caring for the needs of others.

Fast-forward a couple of decades. It was now 2009, and I was facilitating a study with my small group, focusing as usual on the needs of my friends. This study was one I had suggested because it led participants to process their life history and understand the impact their stories have had on their lives. Ironically, I chose this study for the benefit of my friends, since at that time, I was blind to my own needs. Ever the therapist, I sat back, focusing on guiding them to tell their stories. Intent on listening and caring, I thought nothing of what God might want to do in my life. I didn't understand then but know now how often I put on my "therapist" hat to avoid dealing with the mess and pain of my own life. It was safer, right?

One night stands out clearly in my memory, a transformational night that shook me to my core. That night, while reviewing the study with my small group, the question was asked, "During the time of your trauma or loss or abuse, who was there to protect you?" For a moment, I was blank and couldn't think of how this question related to my story. But then it hit me like a shotgun blast to the gut—the answer was *no one,* because my older brother was my protector. When he died, I felt stripped of my protection—and with my parents disappearing into their grief, I felt very much abandoned and alone. I was left at eight years old to fend for myself. A compliant child, I didn't require a lot of attention, and so I became *the forgotten child.*

I was surprised at the intensity of the pain I felt, and I realized that the Lord was leading me into a deeper part of my story—one I hadn't been ready to face earlier in my life. I knew God was supposed to be loving and good and faithful—but in my heart I knew he had abandoned me. I grew up feeling like God was distant and harsh. He chastised me if I was bad but was silent when I needed him. Ever since I was a little girl, I felt like it was up to me to be "good," to try to please God so that I could avoid negative consequences and receive blessings from him, which led to my performance-oriented Christianity. It also led to many masks. You see, I was a fake who tried to pretend to the world that I was good, when underneath my life was seething with sin and shame that was controlling my life.

During a subsequent time of prayer and reflection with my dear friends, God showed me that I had a wall around my heart. Through my friends, I was lovingly challenged to pray about the answers to some questions: What's behind the walls? What caused you to build them in the first place? What will it take to let some of the walls down? What will it look like if you let down the walls? How will you let yourself be deeply loved by God and by others?

And so like the good Christian that I was, I wrote down all the questions—and I promptly put them aside and went back to the serious business of living. After all, I was busy serving God.

Devastating Betrayal

A number of weeks later, I was studying the story of Lazarus and his sisters, Mary and Martha, in John 11:

Now a man named Lazarus was sick. He was from Bethany, the village of Mary and her sister Martha. (This Mary, whose brother Lazarus now lay sick, was the same one who poured perfume on the Lord and wiped his feet with her hair.) So the sisters sent word to Jesus, "Lord, the one you love is sick." When he heard this, Jesus said, "This sickness will not end in death. No, it is for God's glory so that God's Son may be glorified through it." Now Jesus loved Martha and her sister and Lazarus. So when he heard that Lazarus was sick, he stayed where he was two more days. (John 11:1–6)

Now this is the Mary who sat at Jesus' feet when he came to visit, while her sister, Martha, was bustling around serving; this was the Mary who Jesus said had *"chosen what is better"* (Luke 10:42); this was also the Mary who poured expensive perfume on Jesus' feet in an act of worship. She must have adored Jesus and trusted him deeply. But Jesus waited before going to see his friends, and Lazarus died. Jesus then went to see his friends and ended up raising Lazarus from the dead. Many of the Jews put their faith in him as a result of witnessing this miracle.

Now I've heard and read this story many times, but this time I really resonated with Mary. She must have believed deeply in Jesus, so much so that when her brother lay dying, she sent for him, believing that he was their hope. But then her brother died—how shattered she must have been! The One she worshipped had not met her at her point of greatest need. She must have been devastated, because the Scriptures tell us that when Jesus finally came, *"Martha…went out to meet him, but **Mary stayed at home**"* (John 11:20). Imagine her feelings of betrayal, so strong that she stayed at home rather than running out to greet him like she normally would. But Jesus, understanding her pain, pursued her and asked Martha to tell Mary to come out.

This next part of this story really impacted me. Mary immediately got up and quickly went to meet Jesus—*quickly,* meaning without "further delay," without reluctance or fear. She went to meet him, weeping and honest in her pain and anger. She laid it out—her complete disappointment in Jesus. He had let her down.

Rather than being defensive or explaining himself, Jesus felt deeply moved, and he wept. Rather than rebuking Mary for her tears and accusation, Jesus saw beneath her words to her pain and her feelings of betrayal. And he had great compassion for her.

I began to ask myself, "Why do I resonate so much with Mary?" I wrote in my journal,

I, too, lost my brother, even after much prayer. Jesus, you did not heal him. You allowed our family to be shattered. You took away my protector and left me alone, abandoned and scared. You didn't relieve my pain…but you were moved deeply and you wept for me. Today, as I continue to explore the impact of that loss in my life, I am realizing more and more how devastating that loss was for me. Yet you let it happen. That loss, at the age of eight, was when I realized that loving someone didn't keep them safe. I also learned that believing in you didn't protect the people I love. You sometimes take people we love away from us. But like with Mary, even when I stay away from you because I am hurt or feel betrayed by you, you still ASK for me. Even when I'm UGLY in my emotions, you still ask for me. But I have to come to you like Mary did. I have to trust your love enough to come to you, fall at your feet and pour out my heart.

And that was the final straw that broke my resistance and made the walls come down around my heart. I finally cried out to Jesus and began to weep and ask him questions out of the agony of my broken heart: "Why did you let Tim die? Why did you tear apart my family? Why did you leave me alone as a little girl? Why did you leave me so unprotected? Why did you leave me lost in the shuffle of life, grief and loss?" And then the deepest cry of my heart: "Where were you when I needed you?"

New Life

Like Jesus did with Lazarus, he brought forward new life in me. He gave me permission to be gut-honest with him and in so doing helped me be more authentic with him than I'd ever been. And in the midst of all of that ugliness, I felt a palpable sense of his pleasure in me. I don't know how to explain it other than a knowing deep in my spirit of his pleasure in me—not for my "goodness," not for my efforts to please him, not for my service for him, but just because he loves me. And so I allowed that deep sense of God's love for me wash over me; and as I shared the experience with my friends and my husband, I finally began to let down the walls around my heart to the people in my life—I began to show my vulnerabilities to others and receive love in response from them.

Were there answers to my questions? No. But I realized that just in asking the questions I could trust Jesus would weep with me and hurt with me, just as he did with Mary. There was also a peace that I didn't need to know the answers, because he has promised me that I will one day see God's glory in my story.

Like me, when George understood the impact of his own story and allowed himself to *feel* his pain, he began to find his way back. It took great courage on his part—an internal strength far greater than what it took to be a missionary in the field—to face his fear, anguish and broken trust. It was hard work, and many times, he was tempted to run away. All the intense emotions he had hidden away from—anger, betrayal, fear and sorrow—came to the forefront very painfully. But only when he chose to face his pain was he able to heal and open up his heart to his Father. Like limbs frozen by hypothermia, his heart began to thaw out gradually from the gentle warmth of the care he received in my office. With time, his initial throbbing pain gave way to a healthy flow that brought new life.

Digging Deep

So what about you?

If you're beginning to realize your life is crippled because you don't fully trust your Father, is it time for you to re-evaluate God's love and sovereignty? If so, stop and reflect. Take the time *now* to pause and ponder, as long as you need. Don't move on from this point until you can get gut-honest with our Father about all the hidden places in your heart.

What is your story? Where have you experienced loss, trauma or pain? How has that shaped how you see God and his love for you? When was your heart broken, and when has the Lord let you down? And how does that broken trust affect your life today?

Set aside some time to reflect on your story—do it over several occasions if necessary. And pray before you start, something like,

Lord, I come before you, ready to begin exploring my story with you. You know every aspect of my story, all the hidden parts that I haven't even faced or understood. I acknowledge that I'm feeling [afraid, sceptical, wary, etc.—indicate whatever you're feeling right now as you pray], but I choose to open myself to this process. Protect me from the lies of the enemy and help me to hear only your truth. Please help me to remember what you want me to remember, feel what you want me to feel, and hear what you want me to hear. Holy Spirit, come now and guide me as I write my story.

Take your journal notebook or your computer and write down the following headings:

Birth and Infancy

Toddler Years (2 to 4)

Elementary Years (5 to 10)

Early Adolescence (11 to 13)

Teen Years (14 to 18)

Young Adulthood (20s)

Adulthood (30s to present)

Under each of the headings, begin to write down whatever you remember. Don't worry about editing; just allow your words to flow. Reflect specifically on experiences that may have been traumatic or difficult. Think of events that you realize, looking back, have really shaped you. And don't worry about getting this "right"—you will have plenty of opportunities later on to flesh this out more thoroughly. At this point, the key point is to explore your history.

The other important thing to remember is to stay *safe*. If at any point in this exercise you find yourself overwhelmed with emotion, stop and pray, asking the Lord to comfort you and to show you what he wants you to know about that situation. Also, take some deep breaths—in slowly to a count of 4 and then out slowly to a count of 8. Do the deep breathing at least 10 times. If you're unable to bring yourself to a place of equilibrium even after a time of prayer and breathing, stop this exercise and put it aside. Prayerfully consider whether you need to do this exercise in the safety of a therapeutic relationship.

If you, like many others, come from abandonment, betrayal or abuse and have just begun to acknowledge the wounds from your past and are feeling overwhelmed by the emotions, please, I exhort you, don't do this alone. Pray and ask the Lord to lead you to someone who can walk with you through the sorrow, who can hold on to hope for you as you delve into the painful parts of your story that have remained hidden and unexamined. Many people have secretly felt alone for many years and have hidden behind walls. Don't be afraid to reach out to a godly friend, pastor or counsellor who can help you breach the chasm and experience healing love. Relationships where we can be transparent and real with our struggles, where we are accepted fully even in our brokenness, are life-giving. And through that, the Spirit of God flows.

CHAPTER 3

Why Am I So Afraid?

"Fear and trembling seized me and made all my bones shake."

Job 4:14

Giggling, I peeked out from under my blanket, looking for the all-clear signal from my older brother. Catching my eye, he cautioned me to be quiet with a quick shake of his head as he listened to our parents close the door to their bedroom. I held my breath, waiting, until finally he gave us the thumbs up. My sister flung her blanket off and hung over the side of the top bunk bed, ready to start our nightly escapades. I gave her a high-five from the bottom bunk and jumped out of my bed eagerly. My brother, being the eldest, started the circuit; he climbed onto my sister's top bunk, then leapt onto his bed on the other side of our bedroom, glee lighting his face. He then jumped a few times on his bed, slapping his hand on the ceiling every time he was airborne. Crouching down, he jumped onto my bottom bunk, to wait his turn for another round of the course. After my sister went, it was finally my turn. Heart racing, I hesitated, but then I made the leap with my brother's smiling encouragement. I did it!

Before long, our bedroom was a flurry of motion and laughter, blankets and pillows tossed all over the floor, beds squeaking and thumping. We were having such a blast that we didn't notice our door open until it was too late. Our mother's stern face appeared. Busted!

Even as she lectured us, I could see the humour in her eyes, and to this day I swear I heard her laughing as she returned to her bedroom. Looking back, the warmth of this memory wraps its comforting arms around me. It was just me and my beloved family in our tiny apartment, starting hopeful lives in a new country, the land of opportunity. No awareness then of the deadly force about to strike our family. It was a time of simple pleasures and joyful laughter, right before the winds of grief blew the icy storm of winter into our lives, the storm that struck ferociously with the death of my brother when I was eight and then blew relentlessly through my life with three other significant events that same year.

The Loss of Innocence

Her name was Jacqueline, and she was beautiful, with a smile that lit up her entire face. A born leader, she was popular and well-liked by everyone. With her warm nature, she was drawn to underdogs yet strong enough to stand up to anyone who dared to bully her friends. All of that didn't matter to me; all that mattered was that she was my best friend. We spent all of our free time together, giggling and sharing our secrets. But all of that ended the year I was eight.

It's a day carved into my memory. Standing alone on the other side of the street, I watched the moving van drive away with my best friend. My mind was blank, but there was a hollow feeling of panic in my stomach. What was I going to do without Jacquie? Who would be my friend? That was before email and Facebook, so her move to the other side of the country meant the death of our friendship. I didn't cry at that moment; I think I was too numb to know what this loss would mean to me. It was just one more treasured thing that God had taken away from me.

The next day on the school playground, I was lost without Jacquie. I stood there alone, tears welling from my eyes as my heart ached with missing her. Even as the tears poured down my face, I dashed them away quickly, not wanting anyone to see me cry. I had been taught well by my parents to be stoic. With no one to play with, I sought my older sister, who held my hand while walking with me through the playground. Why didn't anyone want to play with me?

That's when the fear of rejection and abandonment began to mark my life. An already shy child, I became even more timid and fearful of reaching out socially. But not wanting anyone to know of my fears, since I thought it would only lead to more rejection, I learned to pretend I didn't care when no one wanted to play with me. I learned to inhabit the space of my imagination to comfort myself, spending hours playing alone with my Barbie doll in my happy imaginary world.

My mother, who was a stay-at-home mom until then, started working full-time to help ease our family's financial struggles. Often left on my own, I felt like I had no one to confide in and no one to care about how I was feeling. I never knew to tell my mom what I was experiencing—she never even knew that my best friend had moved away and that I was lonely and afraid. Sensing my mom's pain after the loss of my brother, I learned to be strong for her so I would not cause her any further hardship. In my child's mind, it was up to me to be her strength and to help her cope with the adversity of life, especially since my father had disappeared into his career and my sister had begun her troubled journey into angry rebellion. That's when the fear of being vulnerable began.

The Final Blow

A few months after my brother died, I became sick with dizzy spells and unexplained symptoms. Alarmed, my parents took me to the hospital, where they kept me for a week of tests to see if I had the same illness that killed my brother. I didn't understand any of that then; I just remember the look of fear on my parents' faces when they took me to the hospital. All I knew was that I was terrified I was going there to die just like my brother. I didn't understand why my parents would leave me alone in the hospital and why they wouldn't come and rescue me. Even after I made repeated frantic phone calls to my parents in the middle of the night, begging for them to take me home, they refused to come. I spent nights crying so hysterically that I would vomit, and I developed a high fever that would not subside because of my emotional trauma. The nurses eventually strapped me into the bed to make sure that I didn't call my parents in the middle of the night or try to escape. I felt all alone with my paralyzing fears, with no one to comfort or care for me. That's when the fear of doctors and hospitals began, as well as a strong reinforcement of the fear of abandonment—the message that I was on my own.

That was when fear grabbed a firm hold of my life and established a vicious stronghold, which lasted for almost 20 years. Over the years, my fears started to control me to the point that I developed ritualistic behaviours to ward off bad luck. I would count things or have to do tasks in a certain order; otherwise something bad would happen. Deep down, I knew that they were irrational, but I continued the behaviours because they helped me deal with my fears and anxiety. Although I was very good at masking my fear, I struggled internally. I was a believer, but my prayers became ritualistic, and I was terrified that if one night I forgot to pray for my loved ones, they would die. But because I spoke to no one about my fears, they grew to the point where they became the fulcrum around which my decisions, emotions and relationships revolved.

As children, our tender and vulnerable spirits expose us to the potential of much pain. Bewildered and unsuspecting, we enter this world vulnerable to the encounters that shape our psyche, our emotional well-being and our relational health. All of us have experienced bumps big and small along the corridors of our childhood, and in the course of those painful experiences we have all made conclusions—oftentimes erroneous—about ourselves, others, the world and even God. Many of us as we grew older feared opening ourselves up to hurt, loss and emotional pain. And once we'd been hurt, we feared ever risking again, and so we closed our hearts protectively and tightened the control on our lives as if we might somehow minimize our exposure to pain. How many of us live with our hearts encased behind walls to protect us from hurt, loss or rejection? We live with the illusion of safety and control, when in reality we are controlled by our fears to the point that we can't surrender to God. And so we live our lives in bondage. Oh, we call it many other things—like being "anal" or a "perfectionist" or "protective" or "careful" or "sensible"—but in the end, all of these things have their roots in fear.

The Deal Breaker

One of my biggest fears is knowing that God allows pain and suffering in our lives. I know it's wrong to believe that God wouldn't let me suffer if he really loved me. This has been a huge stumbling block for me. And so I fear the pain he's allowed and could allow in the future.

I reason that if I really surrender to God, he's going to allow pain in my life to shape me into Christ's character. Growing Christlike character is his will for my life, but I don't want the pain. I don't want to be taken out of my comforts, and I don't want to do the hard work of making changes in my life. And so I can't let go and trust him. For me, this has been one of the biggest deal breakers in my relationship with God and my ability to trust him. *Why does he allow me to suffer?* I don't want that!

I think you may know what I'm talking about.

Because fear is the most powerful force that keeps us in bondage, it often feels impossible to overcome it and do what God is gently calling us to do. Clients often describe a "wall" that seems too huge to overcome, and so they remain trapped behind the prison they've created. And even though the walls begin to cave in on them and feel suffocating, they still choose to remain within. Often they say they "can't" get out, and I must gently remind them that they simply "won't"—that they are choosing to surrender to their fear, rather than to God.

Whatever you choose to surrender to is what—or who—controls you.

Prison of Fear

As I grew into adulthood, I eventually overcame my ritualistic thinking, but I still worried constantly and tried to structure my life to be as safe as possible.

I walked away from the part of God I saw as terrifying and unpredictable. I still prayed, but I was far away from him in my heart. I did not want him messing up my safe life.

But looking back, I can see him reaching out gently to teach me about his grace and love for me and how compassionately he cared for me and understood my fears. He began to show me a side of himself I never knew. In his wisdom (and humour!), God led me to teach a workshop on fear and began to bring clients suffering from anxiety.

And through them, I began to learn that fear is a terrible taskmaster:

• *The more you give into it, the more fiercely it will control your life.*

• *The more you confront it, the weaker it becomes.* I call this the law of the opposites—do the opposite of what you feel you should do when you're deeply afraid, and that fear will begin to lose its power.

• *The less you confront it, it more it grows.* Fear will begin to engulf more and more of your life until it consumes you.

• *Fear seems impossible to overcome.* In actuality, it's a tissue-paper wall that, once you push through, you'll see was not worth the stress and worry. Research shows that only 8 percent of what we fear has any basis in reality. Yet fear-based problems cause the vast majority of emotional issues. The amount of energy and time spent on fear-based thinking is way out of proportion with 8 percent of legitimate concerns!

• *Fear wears masks to hide.* My fear could go underground so that I was unaware that it was controlling me: I'd get defensive when someone was criticizing me; I'd try to control others or situations or keep busy to keep from facing problems. Fear's best mask: eliminating anything and everything that was unsafe or unpredictable so I wouldn't even feel fear. When everything I could possibly be afraid of was out of my life, I could expertly avoid whatever could possibly stimulate the feelings of fear.

• *Fear is the opposite of faith and love.* The more I let fear rule my life, the farther I was from God and faith. I could not grow with God until I learned to deal with my fear. In biblical terms, fear is actually unbelief, and unbelief greatly grieves God's heart. God commands us multiple times in his Word "Do not fear!" He knows it will be our tendency.

After years of personal experience and counselling others, I have concluded that *all* of us struggle with fear—some just hide it better than others. Many have even hidden it from themselves. Fear is likely at the root of stress in our lives.

And God knows this.

Fight or Flight

When we get afraid, we believe that something bad is going to happen to us, and so our adrenal system kicks into gear (and this can turn into a dependency, an addiction). That's our "fight or flight" system that God designed to get us out of danger. However, with fear we often experience mostly "perceived" danger, so we're on high alert to try to prevent the perceived bad thing from happening. But the problem with a constant state of alertness is that our adrenal system gets overused, and that causes our body to begin to break down, resulting in a multitude of problems over the long term.

When we layer on top of that our tendency to overload our lives with too many demands (because we're *afraid* to say no or we're *afraid* that if we don't do it, it won't get done, or we're *afraid* that if we don't, bad things will happen to us), then we create a tremendous amount of stress that our bodies were never designed to bear. When an engine is overburdened by the weight of the load, it eventually breaks down, and sometimes the engine is destroyed altogether. Worse, fear causes a great deal of emotional and relational damage to others—including to our relationship with God, causing us spiritual damage.

Many people cry out to God, asking him to lift their pain and anxiety, but refuse to do *their* part to exercise faith and confront their fear. When we continue to struggle, we blame God and see him as harsh, abandoning us in our hour of need. What we must learn is that God's will is never for us to be struggle-free. Jesus said, "*In this world you will have trouble*" (John 16:33). Character and faith grow by trusting him in the midst of struggles.

I've also learned this about my fear: at the root is my belief that *I* control the outcome of my life. But only God controls the outcomes. Often we trust our ability to control things in our lives, as well as in our loved ones' lives, but it's a total myth. We can't control much of anything or anyone. Unfortunately, we learn to depend on our ability to control outcomes, and when we can't, we panic. We have to learn to transfer our confidence to God. God has given us responsibility, but he's never given us control. We need to stop trying to control what we can't, so that God can.

The Commander of Storms

Remember, we are with the One whom the storm obeys; we are with the One who raised the dead. No storm is beyond God's control, no matter how terrifying and out of *our* control it is. Mark 4:35–41 is a very familiar story, but read it in the context of our struggle with fear: "*That day when evening came, he said to his disciples, 'Let us go over to the other side'*" (Mark 4:35).

Now, we could debate whether Jesus knew a storm was coming. But how many times does God lead us *into* the storm, knowing the fear we'll face? Why would he do that?

"*A furious squall came up, and the waves broke over the boat, so that it was nearly swamped. Jesus was in the stern, sleeping on a cushion*" (Mark 4:37–38).

So here's Jesus snoozing in the middle of a storm. Is he oblivious? Is he foolish? Is God *ever* caught unaware by our storms? Does he say, "Oh, no, I didn't think this would happen! What am I going to do?" Truth: *nothing* is a surprise to God.

But the disciples respond in great fear and anger—and putting myself in their shoes, I know I would respond (and have responded) in much the same way.

"*The disciples woke him and said to him, 'Teacher, don't you care if we drown?'*" (Mark 4:38).

How often do we feel that God doesn't care what we're going through? When we're struggling with a storm in our lives, it gets hard to hear, hard to believe. The word "drown" here actually means "perishing"—how often do we feel that God doesn't care if we die? We equate a lack of change in our circumstances with God's lack of interest. We don't see God acting in the way we want and begin to suspect that he lacks compassion.

"*He got up, rebuked the wind and said to the waves, 'Quiet! Be still!' Then the wind died down and it was completely calm. He said to his disciples, 'Why are you so afraid? Do you still have no faith?'*" (Mark 4:39–40).

When life is out of control, we don't have to be afraid. With us in control, we *will* be afraid—and we should be! Jesus knew that life sometimes would be out of control, but God never is. We have to shift our faith to God.

There's nothing like fear to make us lose our perspective. And once we lose our focus on God, we're dead in the water.

In verse 41 it says the disciples were "*terrified*"—this helped them develop a fear of the Lord, an understanding of how vast Jesus' power was, that even the storms obeyed him. Could Jesus have been teaching the disciples to trust in his character, his sovereignty and love for them, rather than in what he *did* for them? The disciples needed to see that their faith was not in him. How often do we evaluate God's character, promises and love for us by what he *does* for us rather than by *who* he is?

How can we learn to evaluate our circumstances based on God's true character, to learn like the disciples to face our fears with the *fear of the Lord?* He is *able* to do the impossible, and he is far *bigger* than anything we can fear. The disciples went on to do amazing things, facing terrors and great trials, because of their great faith in the One who is *able.*

Remember the story of David and Goliath? The Israelites made a classic mistake that we *all* make, which led them to be terrified of Goliath. They saw Goliath as their problem, and they forgot to factor in God. It was when David entered the picture and saw it as God's problem to deal with—"*the battle is the* LORD's" (1 Samuel 17:47)—that they were delivered. Not that they didn't pray; scared people always pray, and often! But it's a frantic "God fix this; God change that." I call that "worry-prayer," when we spiritualize worry by praying repeatedly for God to deliver us, not really believing he cares—and our fear is the proof that we don't believe.

Be honest with yourself: how many times have you prayed repeatedly for something while feeling great anxiety rather than peace in your heart? How many times have you fretted out loud to God through your prayers? Been there, done that.

Digging Deep

Imagine if fear were not an option in your life. How different would you be? How different would your life be? Listen to the yearning in your soul to know the answer. That yearning is God calling you to go deeper with him.

Begin this process with prayer, asking the Lord to show you your fearful ways. Remember, we're very clever in how we disguise our fears, so make sure you examine all the subtle ways that fear has a stronghold in your life.

> Lord, I confess that I have allowed fear to stop me from trusting you fully. I haven't even admitted to myself how fearful I've been but instead have told myself I'm just being careful or cautious or a perfectionist, or I don't want to hurt people [continue with whatever justifications God brings to mind]. Please show me all the ways that fear has had a stronghold in my life.

As you pray this, write down all the things that God brings to your mind. Remember, he *wants* you to be free of fear, so if you're willing, he will guide you in identifying your strongholds.

As you pray, think through all the times in your life when fear has prevented you from moving forward. Think of all the people, situations and challenges you've avoided because of fear: Was it the confrontation with a friend or co-worker you've been avoiding? Was it in making a much-needed change to your career or job? Was it a school project or exam?

Does fear show itself most in your marriage or relationships? With your kids? Your health? Your finances? Your schooling? Your future?

After you have completed your list of fears, take time to confess and renounce each of these fears to God, asking him to help you overcome their stronghold in your life. Trust him in this: he is just waiting for you to surrender your fears to him.

If your fear has escalated to the point where you're experiencing anxiety, panic attacks, phobias (where you avoid specific things or situations), uncontrollable intrusive thoughts or compulsive behaviours, please reach out for professional help. Ask your doctor or pastor for a recommendation to a reputable therapist who can help you break free from your bondage to fear.

CHAPTER 4

This Is Freedom?

"What good will it be for someone to gain the whole world, yet forfeit their soul?"

Matthew 16:26

The resignation in Max's eyes was obvious, as was the weariness in the hunch of his shoulders. My heart sunk as he told me his story of devastation ripping apart his life.

His wife, the mother of their four young children, had suddenly decided she was tired of being a wife and mother and of all the rules of her church and religion. So she had thrown caution to the wind, moved out, begun an affair with a much younger man, and made her life hanging out at bars with "friends" who were years younger than she was. All in the name of freedom. It was finally her turn, she declared, to do what she wanted.

"The kids will be fine," she lied to herself. In her mind, it was time for them to learn to face real life.

A part of me understood. The restlessness. The fear that she'd missed out. All the years being confined by others. But as I saw the destruction her rebellion wrought upon her family, my heart hurt. Her youngest stayed up nights crying to the point of vomiting. Her second child had regressed to bed-wetting. Her eldest daughter was in and out of trouble at school as she conveyed her inexpressible anger toward her peers. Max was doing everything possible to help his family survive. Bewildered and lost, uncertain of what to do, he'd come to me.

This is freedom?

From the time Adam and Eve considered the possibility of being as powerful and all-knowing as God and the moment they chose to disobey him, they opened the door to rebellion for humanity. They bought into the lie that what was forbidden was better than all the gifts and blessings God had provided so lavishly.

The Fully Lived Life

When God created us, he gave us the freedom to choose whether we would love him, and the freedom to choose not to. But that freedom comes with a price, a price that we sometimes don't realize until it's too late.

Society embraces the right to do anything it wants. The myriad choices offered us reinforce the illusion that living our lives for ourselves is ideal. We choose to throw away old stuff and buy new stuff, we throw away old spouses and get new partners, we throw away babies from our wombs if they are too inconvenient for our lives, or we throw away our jobs and jump ship if something angers us or things don't go according to *our* plans. We regularly protest rules or policies we deem unfair or restrictive and complain about bosses, pastors and leaders. All in the name of freedom and the right to choose.

Underlying this are the sly whispers of the enemy, deceiving us that freedom is about doing whatever we want. And so we resist the gentle voice of our God, who calls us to surrender to him and truly be all he has created us to be. Sure, we've surrendered to let him be our Saviour from suffering for eternity. But we resist letting him be Lord of our lives because of our rebellious spirit and desire to be in control. And this isn't a new thing; people across the ages struggled to be in control, rebelling against all authority, including God. Story after story in the Bible outline this human flaw of ours, as do the history books of humankind.

On My Own Terms

Growing up Christian can often mean formative years of corporal punishment and earning demerits for every possible offence. By the time I was a teen, I had enough of all the rules I knew I had no hope of ever meeting perfectly. Disillusionment set in, and I wanted as little to do with God as possible. I was left to sort through my own issues with all the stresses my parents were dealing with at the time, so I figured it was time to experience the world on my own terms. And my rebellion extended for many years as I tasted many "forbidden fruits" and revelled in my freedom to do whatever I wanted.

When I first started in the career world, I was determined to make my mark, and so I aggressively pursued ambitious goals and financial success. My goal was to have a six-figure income and drive a Mercedes convertible as a mark of my success. I was so determined to have my way, I was known as a "high maintenance girl," and heaven forbid anyone trying to stop me. My focus was only on what I wanted out of life and pursuing that, regardless of what the gentle whisper of the Lord was saying in my long-ignored spirit.

Though I professed to be Christian, I was thumbing my nose at God and ignoring his broken-hearted appeals. In so doing, I was running away from his protection and grace and from my true God-given nature, the calling he had placed on my life to help "*bind up the brokenhearted*" (Isaiah 61:1). Oh yes, I knew about that calling early on in my teens when this verse was given to me during a time of prayer, but like Jonah, I was determined to do my own thing. To heck with all those people I was supposed to bring a message of hope and redemption to. I'd take my chances in the putrid belly of my rebellion!

And yet, in my rebellion, I was the one who suffered, as did the loved ones God had placed in my life and all the people I failed to minister to or witness to during that time. I was so unkind and selfish in those days, no one could distinguish me from nonbelievers. The words from my mouth were often crude and hurtful, and I dropped a number of friends without a thought when they failed to please me or let me have my way. I was impatient and quick to anger when I was displeased, and I was slow to show appreciation for what I felt entitled to have. One of my biggest regrets during that time is how deeply I hurt a dear friend because I could not tolerate the truth she tried to share with me about how I was treating her. I was not teachable in those days (a core value for my life today) because my heart was so hardened with rebellion.

Now when I think back to that time in my life, I remember only the darkness and the bondage, not the so-called "freedom" and fun I was supposed to be experiencing. In fact, much of the shame that held me in captivity when I returned to the Lord was borne out of that time of rebellion. My heart still aches today when I think back to some of the choices I made, mainly because of how I harmed others. I know I am forgiven, but my destructive words and actions can never be taken back. Redemption is possible, I know, but sometimes the jagged shards of our broken relationships can never be restored to their original splendour. How perspective shifts when we're able to look back with clear eyes!

I did not begin to realize who God created me to be or to experience the joy of serving him in my calling until I started the journey back home to him. It was then that he began to show me, with delight, his love for me and who he had created me to be. Now I can *see* the truth of God's calling on my life to care for the broken-hearted in a way that I was too blind and stubborn to see as a youth. And even more remarkable: God has redeemed the stench of my rebellion for good as he has used it to humble my pride and soften my hard heart. Now I come as a broken and forgiven sinner who truly understands *grace*. And as *I've* experienced grace, I can now live it out in my relationships and in my care for others.

Take Max's wife, Sandra, for example: she finally came to my office after living "the high life" with another man for over a year. During that time, she experimented with drugs and sexual promiscuity in her rebellious pursuit of "freedom." But months later she came to see me, broken and desperate, lost in the nightmare of her life. Having witnessed the untold damage she had wreaked on her family, it would have been easy for me to respond to Sandra as her church had done—with rejection and condemnation.

Instead, because of my own journey through the hellhole of rebellion into the light of God's grace, I was able to offer this prodigal daughter what she needed to return home. In the sanctuary of my office, Sandra was finally able to kneel at the altar of grace and cry out for forgiveness. And as she sobbed inconsolably, I saw someone just like me—broken, humbled and in desperate need for God's mercy and love. How could I offer her anything less than what I had received?

And through that simple act of grace, Sandra was able to take the first steps forward to repair her marriage and restore her family. No, it didn't happen overnight; in fact, it required tremendous work and perseverance on her part as well as her husband's, but over time, it was my joy to witness the transformation of this family. Today, this family stands as testimony to the incredible power of God's love to heal and restore us from our worst darkness.

Does Sandra's story speak to you? Do you also long to turn away from your rebellion and return home? Sit with this longing in your heart for as long as you need. Your Father is calling to you. Don't turn away from his love.

True Freedom

In some ways, I wish I could tell you that if you turn back to God, your life will get easier. Wouldn't that be a great tag line to "sell" people on God? In truth, though, after I turned back to God my hardships did not lessen; in many ways, they were more intense. Facing the ugliness in my heart was very painful, as was counting the cost of rebellion on my life. Learning to make better choices was something I had to do baby step by baby step. And taking responsibility for my words and actions, recognizing the eternal impact of my choices—all of that was hard. There were many days where it would have been far easier to give up.

But the strength I received from the Lord to endure and the joy I experienced in obeying him and learning to rely on him was indescribable and gave deep meaning to a life that was previously without real purpose or peace. A life of false freedom, compared to a life of surrender and true freedom with God? There is no comparison in the sense of fulfillment, peace, joy and rightness in my soul. I would never trade that away for anything this world could ever offer me.

Satan would love to convince you that you will lose out if you surrender to God and that your life will turn into one of restrictive rules and regulations. And so he tries to keep your heart hard against God, who knows your heart's longings and wants to give them if you'll abandon yourself to him. Satan warns you with seductive lies that your life won't be any fun and you'll have to suffer if you give up what you think you need. He tempts you into thinking control over your life is your only hope of getting what you need from life.

Yet God's Word says, "*Take delight in the LORD, and he will give you the desires of your heart*" (Psalm 37:4). I know that I have never been more at peace and satisfied with the desires of my heart than when I turned my life back to God. This book, in fact, is one of the fruits of that surrender.

Satan would also love to make that voice of conviction in your heart sound like condemnation and shame. If you gave up your plans it could lead to a changed life. But if he can get you to buy his condemnation, you'll stay stuck in shame, which leads to hopelessness and powerlessness. Satan would love nothing more than to see you continue in bondage to the choices keeping you beyond hope of redemption.

Take it from me: God can use *anything* for good in your life, if you will turn to him and allow his grace to cover you and redeem you. His Word promises, "*And we know that in all things God works for the good of those who love him, who have been called according to his purpose*" (Romans 8:28, emphasis mine). That's a promise from God himself: he will use *all* things for good in our lives, including our sins, our screw-ups, our wrong choices, and our rebellion—everything we could ever do—when we choose to turn our lives over to him.

Digging Deep

How many of us—if we're honest with ourselves—can point to decisions we've made in rebellion that have borne poisonous fruit in our lives and the lives of our loved ones?

What are you running away from? Which relationships are suffering from your unwillingness to be stretched? Be honest with yourself: how has your rebellion cost you and others in your life?

Review your story from chapter 2. Think about all of your experiences and consider where rebellion played a part in your suffering—either the rebellion of someone else or your own. Consider the cost you or a loved one has had to pay.

Think back to the generations before you; is there a generational pattern of rebellion in your family line? What damage in your life right now is a direct result of these generational patterns?

Take the time now to confess all the ways that rebellion has had a hold in your life:

> I proclaim my faith in the True Lord Jesus Christ of Nazareth as my Lord and Saviour. I confess that I have rebelled in the following ways [list all forms of rebellion that come to mind]. Please forgive me, Lord Jesus, and help me to submit myself to you and your ways. Thank you for your grace and love and for accepting me back with open arms.

If you've identified a generational pattern of rebellion in your family, take the time now to confess on behalf of your family and break those patterns, using the following prayer:

> Holy Spirit, please reveal to me now, any known and unknown sins or curses of my ancestors that continue to have a hold upon me and my offspring. [List all sins and curses that God reveals to you on a piece of paper]. I confess the following sins of my ancestors. [Read out all the sins from the list.] I renounce all of the sins of my ancestors. I repent of their unrighteous beliefs, actions and rebellion. I break all rights, grounds or privileges that these sins have had in my life, and I will live under their authority no longer because I belong to Jesus Christ. I place the cross of Jesus Christ between me and each member of my family and all those I have not known or named. By the authority that I have in Jesus Christ, I now command every family and ancestral spirit to be bound in chains and be stripped of all armour, weapons, power, and authority. I command that they return everything that they have stolen from me emotionally, mentally, physically and spiritually now. I ask that God's angels escort them away from me now and take them to Jesus. I invite you, Jesus, to now fill me with your Holy Spirit. I commit to the renewing of my mind, and I align my will with your good and perfect will. All this I do in the name and authority of the true Lord Jesus Christ of Nazareth. Amen.

Don't turn the page without taking the time to reflect. Don't rush through this step just because it might be too uncomfortable to face. Make space in your life to reflect and grieve. Look into the darkness in your heart—not to condemn yourself but *so you may be free.* Grace is waiting for you.

CHAPTER 5

Why Is Nothing Going My Way?

"Anyone who intends to come with me has to let me lead. You're not in the driver's seat; I am. Don't run from suffering; embrace it. Follow me and I'll show you how. Self-help is no help at all. Self-sacrifice is the way, my way, to finding yourself, your true self."

Matthew 16:24–25, MSG

Ann glared at me, furious and disbelieving, so angry that her eyes were bulging and a vein was pulsing in her forehead.

"How dare you tell me I'm wrong about my daughter! There is absolutely nothing wrong with her; she's just lazy and unmotivated and needs to get off her butt and start working harder at school!"

To my chagrin, that meeting ended poorly, as Ann refused to listen after I diagnosed her daughter with a severe learning disability. Instead, she was determined that she had the right idea, and no one could tell her how to raise her daughter. She would—by sheer determination—make her daughter comply and turn things around. After all, who knew her child better than she did?

Needless to say, Ann never came back to my office. Her ears were closed to anything that might challenge her, and her pride caused her to reject possible oversights, mistakes or natural human frailty.

All too often, we think we know best, and in our pride we stubbornly shut out the gentle exhortations of our Father. Too proud to face our weaknesses and mistakes, we make no room for growth or change. When people are bound and determined to remain in the driver's seat, controlling every step of the way, there is very little anyone, even our Father, can do to bring about healing. And that greatly saddens me, as their pride slams shut the door in their Father's face.

Of all the challenges I face in my counselling office, unwillingness to face the truth and pride that keeps up a wall and prevents change grieve me the most. They often are the things that prevent healing in relationships and keep marriages and families in broken pieces. This challenge reminds me time and time again to keep my heart humble and teachable.

Lord, may I *never* turn away from your work that changes me from the inside out!

When Adam and Eve entertained the possibility of being like God, they immediately began imagining how good it would be to have the wisdom of God—oh, to know all that he knows! Scriptures tell us in Genesis 3:6, "*When the woman saw that the fruit of the tree was good for food and pleasing to the eye, and also desirable for gaining wisdom, she took some and ate it*" (emphasis mine). Ultimately, it was Satan's temptation to her pride that cost her so very dearly. She and Adam wanted to be their own source of wisdom and took the very thing that led to their separation from God.

God created us to worship and exalt him, to live in a state of wonder at his majesty and awesome power, and out of that worship to surrender fully to his lordship in our lives. But when we turn our eyes away from him, we will seek to elevate and exalt something else. Many of us want to exalt ourselves. We want to be our own source of wisdom and power, and we want God to step aside and follow *our* will for our lives—to be our "sugar daddy," as my mentor Adrienne says, providing us what we want, whenever we want it.

But when we live to please ourselves and allow our pride to lead, we make a very bad choice. Numerous passages in the Bible tell us of God's displeasure with pride and the consequences of allowing our pride to reign. Leviticus 26:19 says, "*I will break down your stubborn pride and make the sky above you like iron and the ground beneath you like bronze*"; and Proverbs 11:2 reminds us, "*When pride comes, then comes disgrace, but with humility comes wisdom.*"

It's All About Me

In our culture, self-sufficiency and independence are seen as great virtues. Self-sufficiency rather than neediness or dependence generally makes us feel healthy and competent. But what unfortunately happens is that we begin to take ownership of our own talents, and we use them to feed our egos or elevate our sense of self-worth, rather than seeing them as gifts from God for the benefit of others. We also begin to draw away from God, needing him less and less.

The more self-sufficient we become, the more proud we become, the more we forget about God. And this is very bad news. Deuteronomy 8:17–20 warns us,

You may say to yourself, "My power and the strength of my hands have pro-
duced this wealth for me." But remember the LORD your God, for it is he
who gives you the ability to produce wealth, and so confirms his covenant,
which he swore to your ancestors, as it is today. If you ever forget the LORD
your God and follow other gods and worship and bow down to them, I tes-
tify against you today that you will surely be destroyed. Like the nations the
LORD destroyed before you, so you will be destroyed for not obeying the LORD
your God.

My girlfriends and I used to jokingly call ourselves the "Pride Club" because we well knew our struggles with pride. For all of us, successful and strong women each in our own fashion, bowing down to the lordship of God was a daily battle. And it manifested itself in many hidden ways: from taking the credit for successes in our lives to wanting to do things our way, judging others and feeling a need to tell them how they should live, and having difficulty acknowledging our mistakes.

But one of the most insidious and subtle ways that pride controls me is not in obvious boastful and bragging behaviours (which I can well hide with false humility) but in the struggle with sin. I tend to be quite self-absorbed with my faults and failures and endlessly scrutinize myself for any flaws or weaknesses, examining every thought and feeling to ensure that I am a "good Christian." But here, once again, I am relying on myself to be holy and pure, rather than allowing Jesus to be holy and blameless on my behalf. I become, as I often call myself, "mini-holy spirit" for myself, seeking to convict myself and change myself.

Those of us who struggle with shame and self-condemnation are actually struggling with pride, because somehow we believe that our "badness" is too big for God, and therefore we have to take care of ourselves. We also become quite self-absorbed in our own pain and don't reach out to God for healing, focusing instead on ourselves and our "stuff." You see, pride ultimately reveals our focus on self. What we focus most on becomes our idol in our lives, even when it's through excruciating self-consciousness and self-hatred. We become the most important focal point in our lives, leaving little energy or attention for the people God wants us to be his light to. No matter how long I've walked this journey as a Christ-follower, I'm still astounded at the many subtle ways pride insinuates itself into my life and my thinking and how often I deceive myself into thinking that my motivations are genuine or pure.

Into My Own Hands

Prior to my burnout, I wandered for three years in a land I call the *Land of the Unknown*. You ever been there? No matter how often I beseeched God for answers or begged for direction, he remained silent. It seemed he had doomed me to a vast desert with my unanswered prayers and questions. The ironic thing was that it was my own doing that landed me there, a decision to pursue a business opportunity that went sour. But it didn't matter; I was still angry with God for abandoning me.

Ah, the hubris of our egos! I had even convinced myself I was following God's will for my life—who else could lead me to do this grand thing that was going to change the world? My misdirected belief (in myself) made the death of my dream even more painful as I struggled with a sense that I had somehow failed God.

I had partnered with an organization to increase our influence from reaching hundreds to impacting thousands of hurting families. We ignored the advice of every business person we spoke to who doubted the wisdom and pointed out the complexity of what we were planning. Never mind that city zoning and bylaws could bring our ambitious plans to a screeching halt. Forget that my trusted advisors, my husband, my family and my friends had serious reservations. God would pave the way. He was depending on me to do my part for his kingdom!

I look back at the many signs that all was not well with this plan, and I realize that instead of listening to the gentle counsel of the Holy Spirit, I stubbornly kept going, convinced that the hardships we experienced were the cost of following God's will. And the more uphill the journey, the more determinedly I forged ahead, ignoring the growing pain in my heart warning me that what was happening was not right, from the escalating costs that became unmanageable to the many obstacles and the whispered accusations about my motives (oh, that one hurt!). My heart aches to remember it and realize the foolhardy person I was.

In the end, I was left holding nothing but broken dreams. Convinced God had forgotten me and allowed me to trust in empty promises and fickle supporters, I felt utterly abandoned—an all-too-familiar echo of the anguish in my childhood. But rather than facing the pain, I began to push harder. In my pride, my secret woundedness began to drive me to desperate measures.

My many decisions to save the sinking ship were futile attempts to regain a control I never had. I hoped to demonstrate good leadership and proceeded to deceive myself and the world that all I was doing was for God. My enormous lifeboat of pride was quickly sinking, but I kept bailing and paddling with my unwieldy twin oars—Fear of Failure and Need for Validation. Only when I'd sunk, exhausted and panicking, did I finally realize the true cost of all my work. I have never been so utterly discouraged and embittered. All of that effort, and still no results. And in my deeply fearful and unloved heart, I knew God had no love for me. He wasn't there for me yet again.

I had wrenched open doors by sheer determination, but the Lord had allowed door after door to slam shut and I was incensed and devastated. *Why? Does he hate me? Has he set me up, only to withhold any goodness from me? Why does he never come through with what I **really** want?*

I couldn't understand. *Well, fine then,* I finally decided. *I guess getting what I want is all up to me.*

Can you imagine the painful time that followed? Every day, gritting my teeth to go to work, pretending all was well, drunk on the toxic wine of denial, then unable to keep up the pretense and going home many nights in tears. There were sleepless nights when I was gripped by anxiety so fierce that I could feel the panic biting the edges of my sanity. Pushing my fears down only caused my mood to explode in unreasonable anger over the smallest grievance. But as was my habit at that time, I coped by withdrawing. *Alone,* rang the familiar clang from my childhood. Numb and exhausted, I sleepwalked my way through life at work and home. And when the dream came to a bitter end, I was left with all the broken pieces. All that effort and sacrifice, and for what?

Let It Be with Me as You Say

I love the story of Mary, the mother of Jesus. As a young girl she encountered an angel who went on to tell her that she would be bearing the Son of God, even though she was a virgin and would surely face public condemnation and judgment. That wasn't her plan when she woke up that morning; nor was it something she even contemplated as she planned her future with Joseph. Who knows what dreams or hopes she carried in her heart, what plans she had for her life. But I love her response to God's invitation to be a part of his bigger story in the history of mankind: *"Let it be with me just as you say"* (Luke 1:38, MSG). And with those words, she surrendered her plans, her dreams, and her control over her life—not in a minor way, mind you, but in a big-time way. And 33 years later, her son Jesus, as he faced the cross, said a similar thing to his Father, *"I'm ready. Do it your way"* (Matthew 26:42, MSG).

Do it your way, Father.

I almost missed it the first time. It was a weekday morning, just before I was heading off to work. I was doing my devotions, mindlessly reading the familiar story of Mary's encounter with the angel. It just happened to be the chapter of the Bible I was in. But thinking ahead to the busy day ahead of me, I didn't pay it much heed. My anxiety had a far greater pull on my attention. My spiritual life was pretty dry at this point, but I wasn't willing to face how my bitter disappointment had shut my heart down. And so I was just going through the motions. For some reason that day, something caused me to stop, made me read the passage again. And it jumped out at me: *"Let it be with me just as you say."*

As I sat with that phrase for a moment, a myriad of emotions raced through me. Resistance. Guilt. Self-criticism. Sorrow. But through that, a dawning realization. My stomach began to unknot. I began to feel a lightness in my spirit as I felt the Lord speaking to me through Mary's story. I felt a sense of conviction, and everything in me began to let go. *Yes, Papa, let it be with me as you say!*

It was only when I stopped fighting God that I was able to shift from my singular focus on what I wanted. It was then that my perspective began to change. Maybe he did have a better plan in store for me. Maybe he was protecting me from some greater pain. When I stopped interpreting the closed doors as God's denial of what I wanted, I began to see the setbacks as his way of leading me to his best for me.

I am grateful for my Father's gracious patience as he allowed me to travel to the end of myself. He wasn't "hanging me out to dry" as I thought he was; instead, he was allowing me to experience the life I wasn't meant to live—a life of foolish and short-sighted choices rooted only in my pride, woundedness and self-deception. I am thankful that he shut those doors in his protection and love for me, knowing me best and knowing his good plans for my life. I am in awe of where he led me, out of the arid desert to the life-giving oasis in that same land.

Same land—but very different experience.

I now know that my Father is the designer of this land. He's the writer of the story, and I am experiencing a peace and anticipation for what he's doing in my life. He was only waiting for me to let go and surrender. When I returned, pride in hand, broken and battered for having gone my own way, he responded in joy, wrapping around me the robes of royalty and celebrating my return by calling for the fatted calf and inviting everyone for a serious party (not to mention the jewelry—my friends know I love bling!).

When we fail to surrender to God, we rely on ourselves—the selves we have elevated to being gods in our lives. And God, in his infinite grace and wisdom, allows us the pain of our self-worship so that we may come to the end of ourselves and come back to the worship and lordship of God. Are you experiencing that pain in your life today? Could God be calling you back with love and tenderness, back to surrendering to a right worship of the one true God?

Digging Deep

Are you in the Land of the Unknown? Are your prayers returning void? Are your plans falling apart, or is life not turning out the way you intended? Pause and take the time to be honest about this and how you've been reacting to the wrestling of control from your hands. Have you been fighting your Father?

Where are you refusing to surrender control of your life? Look at the pain points of your life today, the areas that cause you the greatest stress, anxiety and worry—could God be asking you to surrender to him in that area? Is it in your marriage? Your singleness? Your children? Your childlessness? Career? Finances? Health? Think about the unanswered prayers that cause you the greatest anxiety or disappointment—is God asking you to surrender this to him?

Choose one of the following:

1. Read Mary's story in Luke 1:26–38. Put yourself in Mary's shoes and imagine an angel coming to you to turn your life upside down. Picture the scene in your mind. Where are you standing, and where is the angel? What do you see, hear or even smell? Think about how you would feel; imagine what would be going through your mind. As you read through the passage again, write down which phrases jump out at you. What is God trying to tell you through those phrases, this passage?

2. You may find it easier to connect with Joseph's story in Matthew 1:18–24. Put yourself in Joseph's place and imagine an angel coming to you in a dream. Consider what you would feel. What details jump out at you as you read the passage again? What questions would be racing through your mind? What doubts and fears? And think about what led Joseph to obey. Now ask the Lord to show you what's on his mind for you as you ponder this passage.

Remember, the Land of the Unknown can be an arid desert where bitterness, blame, anger and fear push their thorny branches through the dry, rocky soil to choke out life. Or it can be an oasis, a lush and fruitful place that births a new life of hope, peace, and joy. You choose.

CHAPTER 6

Why Can't I Just Believe?

So we see that they were not able to enter [the Promised Land], because of their unbelief.

Hebrews 3:19

I sat in my car, so angry that I had to use every ounce of my strength to hold back my screams. My hands were shaking so hard from the effort that I could not start the car. I sat there for a few minutes, taking deep breaths to try to calm myself before driving, tears streaming down my face. I could not believe it. The deal had fallen through, even though I was sure that this time would be it. The property I was determined to purchase—even though it was hundreds of thousands of dollars above my original budget—would not be mine. Hunching over the steering wheel, I felt the weight of my failure once again on my shoulders. What would I tell my team? They were counting on me. I had already cost them so much when they willingly followed me into our failed business venture. How could I ever make it up to them?

And now I had failed them again.

Coming on the heels of the business disaster we had just experienced, this was one more devastating disappointment. Starting to rebuild my business, I had grand visions of beginning again in a beautiful new location. But after a year and a half of searching and viewing multiple properties, I had yet to find us a new home. Time was ticking away. People were starting to wonder. Discouragement amongst the team was high. The enormous responsibility I carried was like a dead weight on my back. Even as I tried to run to the finish line on behalf of the team, the weight of their expectations and disappointments caused me to stumble and fall short time and again.

But really, if I was honest with myself, this wasn't about my team. This was about the One who had really failed me. Yet again, God had slammed the door shut on what I desperately wanted; it was just one more confirmation that I couldn't count on him, that he was always going to let me down. Sure, he was supposed to be good and loving, but at that moment I doubted whether any of it was really true.

Completely absorbed by my anger and disappointment, I could not see beyond my sense of God's betrayal to what he was showing me. The deep roots of unbelief in my life were fuelled by my bitter conclusions every time God failed to come through for me. My inability to fully trust God—based on my negative interpretations of my circumstances—drove me further and further away from surrendering to him. My unbelief had deepened the wedge in my heart against him, and in that I could not experience any peace. I could only continue my desperate attempts to reason and figure things out for myself.

Just as Adam and Eve's fatal choice in the Garden of Eden demonstrated their unbelief, so too did my response show that I did not believe in God's goodness. John Piper, in his book *A Godward Life,* describes Adam's failure:

> Adam failed because he did not trust the grace of God to pursue him with goodness and mercy all his days (Psalm 23:6). He fell for the lie that God was holding back some really good thing and that he could decide on his own what was "good and evil." Faith does not do that. Faith is the assurance of things hoped for (Hebrews 11:1). It is the confidence that God withholds no good thing from us (Psalm 84:11). It is the firm hope that God works for those who wait for him (Isaiah 64:4) and will meet all our needs according to his riches in glory (Philippians 4:19).[2]

Is God Holding Out on Me?

How often we look at our lives and, when we see that it's not all we want it to be, wonder at God's goodness. When we suffer or miss out on something we've desired for so long, we question his provision and his love for us. And in our unbelief and doubt, we reach out and grab for ourselves the forbidden fruit, certain that this is our only chance to get what we want. Because certainly, we can't count on God to come through for us. Many of us—right now—are living out the direct consequences of our choice to reach out and grab the forbidden fruit. But in our anger and sense of betrayal, we blame God for all of our suffering. I know that personally, but boy, is that a hard truth to swallow! I'd much rather doubt God, take care of things myself, and then blame him when things go wrong.

I have walked this reality for myself, and I have also counselled countless people who came to me when they were bearing the consequences of the choices they made to reach out to forbidden fruit—to break their marital vows, to cut corners in their financial decisions, or to pursue pleasures that ultimately wrapped their addictive tendrils around their lives. And some of these consequences are lifelong. My work with them is in helping them to bear up under the pain and discover God's grace and love through that pain.

God never intended us to suffer from the consequences of unbelief. But when we reach for anything other than God himself to be our sustenance, our failure to believe in God's goodness prevents the very blessings and abundance God longs to rain down on us.

Can you see the schemes of the enemy in this? And can you see how, even in them, God's grace redeems our suffering if we let it? Will you trust that if you choose to humble yourself before him and surrender your unbelief to him, there is freedom from pain that you can experience?

I confess, even as I write these words, I grapple with unbelief in my own life right now. I struggle with turning away from God when I am hurting. I continue to seek out my sense of worth in my achievements and in the fickle praise of men. But like scarce rain drying quickly in the hot desert sun, this source runs dry. Even as I seek water from this mirage, the illusory oasis disappears before I can reach it, leaving me thirsty and dying for more. I leave empty yet again.

But God has shown me what's at the root: I don't truly believe he can help me. I don't fully trust in his love—could he really still love me? How can I depend on him?

And that's where the trouble lies. If I don't believe he'll come through for me then I have no choice but to rely on myself.

The God of Common Sense

God has given us a great gift in our ability to reason and problem-solve. But in our Western science-based world, we have elevated our intellect to godlike status. And so we don't believe in something we can't understand or analyze. What doesn't make "sense" to our rational minds we dismiss because we can't fit it into our intellect.

Even in Christian circles, we talk about "wisdom" and "common sense" as if they were interchangeable. They are not. God defines wisdom as the knowledge he gives to us. Proverbs 2:6 says, *"For the LORD gives wisdom; and from his mouth come knowledge and understanding."* Common sense, on the other hand, is knowledge common to people, derived from our experiences.

Oswald Chambers describes this problem in *My Utmost for His Highest:*

Every time you venture out in your life of faith, you will find something in your circumstances that, from a common sense standpoint, will flatly contradict your faith. But common sense is not faith, and faith is not common sense. In fact, they are as different as the natural life and the spiritual. Can you trust Jesus Christ where your common sense cannot trust Him? Can you venture out with courage on the words of Jesus Christ, while the realities of your common sense continue to shout, "It's all a lie"?[3]

A number of years ago, I was involved in planning an event that took months to organize. Then shortly before the event was to occur, a health crisis occurred that caused people to worry whether it was safe to continue with the event. Nationwide, people were being advised to avoid large crowds for fear that this could cause the deadly virus to spread. Fear grabbed a hold of countless people, causing many to overreact and hide away at home, avoiding work, church and social functions; kids were being pulled from schools, and events were being cancelled because of poor attendance.

While this struck fear into our hearts, our committee spent time in prayer, and we felt that the Lord was telling us to continue, in spite of all that was going on. Ironically, the theme of our event was related to courage and faith, and we felt our faith being tested. At the same time, we knew that we had to be wise and put safeguards into place to ensure safety for our attendees. Based on the guidance given to us by medical personnel, we put into place procedures that would minimize the risk of exposure. We knew that faith in God didn't mean being careless, that we were to use our minds to research, gain understanding and then take steps. Do our part, and then trust God with the outcome.

With a few days left before the event, a leader in our church contacted me and strongly urged us to cancel or, barring that, forbid health care workers from attending, since they were the ones most likely to be exposed to this virus where they worked. When I told her doing so would greatly hurt a number of women in our church who were working hard to care for others, she persisted in presenting the "data" to show me that we were being foolhardy in our decision to continue. I tried to explain the steps we were taking to protect the attendees, as well as the research we ourselves had done, but she wouldn't listen. Finally, I suggested trusting God and taking a leap of faith. I'll never forget her response.

"Well God did give you a brain, didn't he? And he wants you to use it and show some common sense!"

I must confess I handled that situation very badly. And in the process, I sinned against that leader and caused her unwarranted pain by my words and actions. But deep within my heart, I struggled with how easily faith is confused with a lack of common sense, irrationality and even irresponsibility. How hard it is to live by faith in our rational world! How often is the fear that holds us back from a great act of God called "common sense"?

I'm not suggesting that we throw away our common sense. We are commanded by God to use our minds, and he has given us the wonderful gift of our intellect to explore, understand and make good decisions. But common sense needs to be balanced with our faith. Too often, we slide too far one way, refuse to exercise any common sense, and call that faith—like the believer who chooses not to pursue medical treatment because she believes that faith alone will heal her cancer. Or we take things too much into our own hands, and if we can't see it, touch it or have "data" to back up our decision, we refuse to trust God—like the doubter who refuses to tithe because he can't see how God will provide for him to pay his bills.

But one of the biggest barriers to a life of fullness with God is our unbelief. Time and again we refuse to surrender to God, because his call doesn't make sense. It's too *unbelievable.* And our unbelief keeps us from making that leap of faith. In our educated world, we don't even realize how deeply in bondage we are to unbelief and how little we have because of our lack of faith. *"[Jesus] did only a few miracles there because of their unbelief"* (Matthew 13:58, NLT). Aren't we losing out on the Lord's "mighty works" in our lives because of our unbelief?

Digging Deep

Get honest with yourself: how often have you relied on your intellect and "common sense" instead of faith?

In what areas of your life does unbelief reign? Your marriage? Your children? Your work? Your health? Your dreams and desires? Your sin struggles? Ask God to show you where you've secretly believed that nothing will ever change in an area of your life.

And ask him for the faith to trust him to take over.

CHAPTER 7

Why Am I So Burnt-Out?

"You are like whitewashed tombs, which look beautiful on the outside but on the inside are full of the bones of the dead and everything unclean."

Matthew 23:27

A friend of mine has been struggling with his faith, to the point that he's questioning whether God is even real.

A former faithful pastor who was passionate for Christ, Darren left what he thought was his calling, only to slowly languish, trapped for years in the Land of the Unknown. After a number of tremendously wounding experiences with fellow Christians and leaders—as well as a growing sense that he did not fit into the safe and tidy box of what a "good" Christian looks like—this friend of mine began to question many of his core beliefs. Observing the abuse and damage done in the name of Jesus Christ and feeling bitter and disheartened by the hypocrisy and lack of authenticity of the religious people around him, Darren was one step away from giving up on his faith all together.

If this was what following Jesus meant, he didn't want anything to do with it.

Contrast this with Jane, who grew up in a strict Christian home and faithfully adhered to all the rules of her faith, never questioning the expectations that had been placed upon her. When minor troubles hit her safe and uneventful life, she simply smiled and said the trite phrases that Christians say to themselves, such as "God is faithful," convincing herself that she was "fine." In conversations with Jane, I felt like I never really knew her heart, because she was so quick to quote Scripture verses and keep up the religious front. And more heartbreakingly, I sensed that she didn't truly connect to the truth of God's love for her and her identity as his beloved daughter beyond a superficial nod to the empty words she quoted.

My heart ached especially for Jane because I knew that when the winds of storms came into her life—you know that kind that has the power to knock us senseless—her shallow faith and deadened heart would fail her. Ironic that where she was unwilling to go now was precisely where she will end up—questioning her faith and believing that God has left her when her pain is unrelenting in spite of prayers. Without a willingness now to look honestly at the disconnect between her beliefs and the reality of the pain that God allows in our lives, I feared for her ability to handle crises when they later came.

The deepest sadness for me was that Jane wouldn't encounter the real and living God in her neat and tidy Christian life shored up by the empty strength of the rules of her religion rather than built on the rock-solid foundation of a genuine relationship with her Father. And if I had to be honest with myself, I would have much rather spent time with Darren than with Jane, even when he was spewing vitriolic words and questioning the truth of God's Word. Darren on a rant was preferable to Jane in her superficial and saccharine serenity. At least he was being honest.

The truth is, I was Jane at one point in my life. Proud of all the Scriptures I had memorized, content in all the ways I was disciplined enough to pray and read my Bible (unlike many of the struggling Christians I judged around me) and self-satisfied with the times I was able to resist sin and take the "higher road," I felt it was my duty to stand firm for my faith and be a witness for Christ to the world. My bookshelves were full of books teaching me how to be godly, all underlined and highlighted to help me remember all I had to do. I didn't realize I was heading towards a huge tumble off the precipice of pride, a sustained time in the desert far away from God. Isn't such a fall inevitable when you can't sustain your level of effort? My motivations were genuine. I wanted to be obedient to God, but in my pride and attempts to be holy in my own strength I lost sight of what it really means to follow Christ.

It was only when I realized how completely parched my soul was and how deeply I still struggled with insecurities about my value as a child of God—especially with, if I was honest with myself, my constant failures in following the rules (the good old sin-confess cycle)—that I began to recognize that something was missing in my walk with God. It was only when I realized how much of my life was based on drudgery and empty obedience that I started to question my faith journey. It was only when I recognized how hard my heart had become and how judgmental I was becoming about other struggling Christians around me that I awoke from the religious fog I was in. I thank God for his patience and grace with me as he broke through my pride and religiosity to woo me to him. And thank God that through his love for me in many intimate times together that I was able to experience an awakened heart and freedom from religious rules.

Beyond Religion to Relationship

A number of years ago, I picked up *The Shack* by William P. Young after hearing all the controversy about it. I wondered why so many religious leaders were denouncing it, some even saying it was an instrument of the devil. I soon understood why: in his almost irreverent style, Young painted a startling picture of God the Father, Son and Holy Spirit, one very contrary to what is often preached from the pulpit. I was quickly enthralled, it coming as it did when I was just beginning to understand the bondage I was in of religious effort and pride. It was a book the Lord used in my search for something *more,* something to explain the emptiness in my heart.

Those who could approach it as fiction and get beyond the obvious theology issues and questionable depictions of God found, as I did, a resonating message of God's love and his anti-religious, pro-relationship idea of life simply living loved by him. The protagonist, Mack, dialogues with Jesus, who shatters his view of Christianity when he says, "I don't create institutions; that's an occupation for those who want to play God. So no, I'm not too big on religion."[4] Instead, Jesus says he prefers the "simplicity and purity of enjoying a growing friendship...of sharing this journey together."[5]

Further on in the story, Sarayu (the character representing the Holy Spirit) explains to Mack,

> "The Bible doesn't teach you to follow rules. It is a picture of Jesus. While words may tell you what God is like and even what he may want from you, you cannot do any of it on your own. Life and living are *in him* and in no other...Religion is about having the right answers, and some of its answers are right. But I am about the process that takes you to the *living answer,* and once you get to him, he will change you from the inside."[6]

That was revelatory to me as I learned how rule following—with all of its "noble" sounding expressions like "responsibility" and "expectations"—was a way for me to stay in control. And with the lingering tendrils of fear in my life, I craved certainty and an assurance that I was okay in God's eyes. Pride, yes, but also fear kept me in bondage to my religion—the religion that would never let up on all I had to do to meet what I perceived to be God's expectations of me.

And so it was like a "get out of jail free" card when I read Young's picture of relationship with God through what he had God say to Mack:

"If you and I are friends, there is an expectancy that exists within our relationship…[an] expectancy of being together, of laughing and talking. That expectancy has no concrete definition; it is alive and dynamic and everything that emerges from our being together is a unique gift shared by no one else. But what happens if I change that 'expectancy' to an '*expectation*'—spoken or unspoken? Suddenly, law has entered our relationship. You are now expected to perform in a way that meets my expectations. Our living friendship rapidly deteriorates into a dead thing with rules and requirements…Responsibilities and expectations are the basis of guilt and shame and judgement, and they provide the essential framework that promotes performance as the basis for identity and value."[7] (emphasis mine)

A dead thing with rules and requirements. No wonder shame and judgment marked my "relationship" with God when I saw him as the author of the responsibilities and expectations that trapped me in performance.

The "Gospel of Sin Management"

That's when it struck me: how much of my Christianity was based on tasks, obligations and "shoulds"? All the things I thought I *ought* to do and believe— they were well-meaning, certainly, but I realized that in my religiosity I was essentially cutting God out of my life, telling him that I didn't need him, that it was up to me to do the Christian walk. And the fruit of this? Enormous pride, self-righteousness and a parched spirit, secretly weary yet having to maintain the mask of a "good Christian." I was trapped, unable to experience or understand my Father's heart. It was when I finally began to let go of my religious self-effort and performance-based Christianity that I began to experience Jesus as the true Living Water, which began to soothe and restore my dry, weary spirit.

"You have your heads in your Bible constantly because you think you'll find eternal life there. But you miss the forest for the trees. These Scriptures are all about me! And here I am, standing right before you, and you aren't willing to receive from me the life you say you want." (John 5:39–40, MSG)

Dallas Willard says in *The Divine Conspiracy,*

History has brought us to the point where the Christian message is thought to be essentially concerned only with how to deal with sin: with wrongdoing or wrong-being and its effects. Life, our actual existence, is not included in what is now presented as the heart of the Christian message, or it is included only marginally.[8]

Thus Dallas describes the gospel we have today as "gospels of sin management." Sin is the problem, and Christianity is the cure. Knowing what's right—getting our doctrine right—and living it out in our lives becomes our primary focus. It becomes not just our way of life but the *source* of life. But notice this: the Pharisees knew more about the Bible than most of us ever will, and it *hardened* their hearts. Knowledge just isn't all it's cracked up to be.

And because we are ever-inventive, it's not enough that we follow the rules of the Bible religiously; we have to rewrite the Law to emphasize things that we don't think too highly of. *No Dancing Allowed. No Playing Cards Allowed. No Secular Music.* And if that finger-shaking isn't enough, we add in all the things we have to do in exchange for approval from heaven: *Thou must serve every Sunday, Wednesday and Friday. Thou must read the Bible daily for at least an hour.* God is now seen as the obsessive tax auditor eager to find fault with anybody and everybody.

Jesus Came to Fulfill the Law

There's an important distinction here, critical to our understanding of what Jesus meant in chastising the religious leaders of his time. Sometimes, in our fervent attempts to focus on God's grace rather than legalistic religiosity, we swing too far the other way and forget the importance of the law in God's eyes. In confronting the Pharisees, Jesus was denouncing their self-righteousness, effort, moral preening, and hypocrisy; he was confronting them on a form of religion that was all law and no grace.

People hear "religion" and think of rules, rituals, dogma, and institutions. People love Oprah and spiritual, not religious, bumper stickers because our North American culture wants a safe, comfortable God who comes without the strictures we associate with traditional Christianity. But the offering of forgiveness and grace was never to remove the law—it was to fulfill it, and that's very different. Jesus is the answer to our inability to fulfill God's law on our own. Jesus did not come to abolish the Law or the Prophets, but to fulfill them (Matthew 5:17). He founded the church (Matthew 16:18), and he established church discipline (Matthew 18:15–20). He instituted a ritual meal (Matthew

26:26–28), and he told his disciples to baptize people and to teach others to obey everything he commanded (Matthew 28:19–20).

The grace that forgives is also the grace that transforms—and it is a grace that transforms us from the inside out. Following Jesus is more than keeping rules, but it's not less. Be honest about your brokenness. It's not about giving up and sinning freely; instead, it's in that acknowledgement of our brokenness that we realize our desperate need for Christ and that we can humble ourselves before him. There is no inherent dignity in being broken in and of itself. Jesus likes the honesty that acknowledges sin, hates it and turns away, but he does not love authenticity for its own sake. When Paul boasted of his weakness, he was boasting of his suffering, his lack of impressiveness, and the trials he endured (1 Corinthians 2:3; 2 Corinthians 11:30; 12:9). He never boasted of his temptations or his sins. That's not what he meant by weakness. Being broken is not the point, except to be forgiven and changed.

The Gift of Rest

The season after my burnout was a time of deep reflection, solitude and quiet time with God. I really had no choice; I was forced to my knees by the Lord using the circumstances of my life to take me to the end of myself. After too many years of wandering the desert, I was done. But I felt horribly trapped by the entangled web of responsibilities, expectations and rules I had set for my life, all the things I thought I *should* do. Quietly, lovingly, inexorably, the Lord began to release me from my burdens, one by one—work, ministry, daily responsibilities—all things I had thought impossible to ever give up, things I felt I had no choice but to continue bearing, regardless of the personal cost. Even while I felt forced to let go out of exhaustion, deep down I sensed God transforming my heart and life.

I retreated completely, away from Christian community (although Hebrews 10:25 rang guiltily in my mind: *"[Do] not [give] up meeting together, as some are in the habit of doing"*). I was so tired of trying hard to be a good Christian, and I wasn't capable of facing other believers' judgments of my failure to meet their expectations. Reading John Ortberg's book *The Me I Want to Be,* I felt the last shackle of my "Christian responsibilities" fall away:

Maybe you have been attending church for years out of a sense of obligation. You show up week after week out of habit, or because someone expects you to, but it is actually increasing the distance between you and God. So here is an idea: stop going to church. Wait until you want to go again. Find out why you want to go. Trust that if you truly seek, God will bring the desire back to you."[9]

And so I did. I stopped attending church altogether for six months.

During that time, I felt so free. Oh, to spend time with the Lord listening to his heart for me, to allow him to love and care for me, to allow others to minister to me, to break free from the rules and religious "expectations"! And so I began to wonder: what would life be like if this is how I lived, without the "excuse" of being physically and emotionally ill? Could this be what Jesus meant when he said the following?

> *"Are you tired? Worn out? Burned out on religion? Come to me. Get away with me and you'll recover your life. I'll show you how to take a real rest. Walk with me and work with me—watch how I do it. Learn the unforced rhythms of grace. I won't lay anything heavy or ill-fitting on you. Keep company with me and you'll learn to live freely and lightly."* (Matthew 11:28–30, MSG)

Digging Deep

What about you? Are you tired of living in bondage to your version of religion Jesus never intended? Are you weary from all your effort? Are you fearful of disappointing God and others and maintaining an empty shell of duty and work?

Take the time now to examine how you live out your faith, as religion or as relationship. Ponder the way you see God—as a God of *expectancy* or a God of *expectations*. How has your view of God shaped the way you live out your faith?

CHAPTER 8

Do I Have to Be a Phony?

"For we have made a lie our refuge and falsehood our hiding place."

Isaiah 28:15

Sara laughed as she told me about her latest fiasco with her three children in the supermarket, describing the mess in aisle 3, where her kids had been fighting over who got to hold the jar of pickles for Mommy. She was laughing so hard that she could barely speak while describing the horrified silence that occurred when the jar came crashing down and the pickles, pickle juice and glass went flying all over the place, splashing annoyed customers in the vicinity. As she told me about the incident, I looked closely at her eyes and noticed that there was no humour there, only a blank fatigue, and I saw the weariness in the set of her hunched shoulders.

As she moved on to share another "hilarious" incident that demonstrated her ineptness as a mother, I interrupted her and asked her softly, "Do you ever get tired of faking it?" Shocked by the question, Sara fell silent, and as she sat there, tears began welling up out of her eyes. She looked at me without words but then nodded, quietly weeping, laughter long forgotten.

Initially Sara had come to my office because she was feeling "blue" and wondered if it was simply postnatal depression that was lingering on longer than she'd experienced with her first two children. A young mother who had dreamt all her life of getting married and having a family, she could not understand why she wasn't feeling more joy living out her dream come true, and she was hoping to gain a few strategies to help her cope better. She was also married to a wonderful husband who loved her, but he was so busy in full-time ministry and travelling for days at a time that she didn't want to burden him with her "minor problems." So she decided at the recommendation of her friends to come for counselling to "fix" herself.

In counselling, as she paused long enough to begin paying attention to her inner world, we began to peel off the roles, duties to perform and "shoulds" that had long governed her life. As she stilled and became honest about how she was feeling, she was finally able to acknowledge her exhaustion and weariness at pretending everything was okay. In fact, she'd been feeling very lonely, abandoned and like a complete failure as a mother for a long time.

A Recovered Faker

Like many Christians, Sara was afraid that if she acknowledged her inner turmoil she would be a "complainer." She maintained she had so much for which to be thankful. She feared disappointing God, whom she thought commanded her to be "joyful always," even in times of difficulty, so she stuffed her feelings down to keep going, pasting a smile on her face. She learned to hide by laughing and making light of her challenges.

Worst of all, Sara began to believe her own marketing and lost touch with her heart, her real self. Having ignored her true feelings so long, she thought all she needed was to "snap out of it." But little by little, like when heavy pancake makeup slowly melts off the face of a stage actor under hot lights, her true face began to show through. As we continued to meet and she learned I was a recovering faker myself, she removed the layers of pretend selves and saw the grime of her hidden shame, wounds and sins covering the woman God had created.

A recovering faker has to fight the temptation to take the easier road of folly. One recent morning, I woke feeling depressed and exhausted, but I decided to begin journaling praise and worship to God in an attempt to forget my misery. After a while of this, I felt a gentle interruption: "My child, worship is only real when it's for me, not as a guard against self-centredness. You are where you are— be there. That is the 'right thing,' coming exactly as you are."

Immediately convicted, I began to write the truth:

Thank you, Lord! That forced worship was about myself. I want a heart of worship and awe for you. Forgive me. I am weary of pretending. Here I am, Lord, naked before you—you love me that way and offer me grace—so undeserved. I can't pretend with you any longer—I don't want to anymore.

And right there, he urged me to rest in him, just as I was.

I wasn't always aware of my forcing. But I saw my condition described perfectly by Simon Tugwell in *The Beatitudes: Soundings in Christian Tradition:*

We hide behind what we know or feel ourselves to be (which we assume to be unacceptable and unlovable) behind some kind of appearance which we hope will be more pleasing. We hide behind pretty faces which we put on for the benefit of our public. And in time we may even come to forget that we are hiding, and think that our assumed pretty face is what we really look like.[10]

But even more sobering, I had no idea of the extent to which this hiddenness skewed my life or the degree to which it had its grasp on my life as *sin*. Thomas Merton commented on this human condition so revealingly:

My false and private self is the one who wants to exist outside the reach of God's will and love—outside of reality and outside of life. And such a self cannot help but be an illusion. We are not very good at recognizing illusions, least of all the ones we cherish about ourselves...A life devoted to the cult of this shadow is what is called a *life of sin*.[11] (emphasis mine)

If You *Really* Knew Me

Faking your way through life is believing that if you let people know the *real* you, they won't like you. Maybe it seems that nothing you do is ever enough. The tapes that play in your head say that if people *really* knew what was going on inside you, they would lose respect for you. Maybe you keep trying to pretend to make others happy, including God, and you are exhausted, physically, emotionally and spiritually. While you play those roles, juggling those masks you have to wear and hiding your pain—especially as a Christian—the pressure increases to keep pretending you have it all together.

Consider the cost to our souls when we do this, the loss of ourselves. Curtis and Eldredge write in *The Sacred Romance*:

Very seldom are we ever invited to live out of our hearts. If we are wanted, we are often wanted for what we can offer functionally: if rich, we are honored for our wealth; if beautiful, for our looks; if intelligent, for our brains. So we learn to offer only those parts of us that are approved, living out a carefully crafted performance to gain acceptance from those who represent life to us. We divorce ourselves from our hearts and begin to live a double life.[12]

I decided to become a psychologist when I was in grade 7. I believed it was the Asian thing to do—become a doctor. Since I couldn't handle the sight of blood, I thought this would do. And when I first started counselling, my motivation was to be a "do-gooder," to serve God and to feel good about myself. It was self-centred. Much of my motivation sprang from my performance-oriented focus. Because of that, I had to be "on" at all times and continually working hard to make everyone "love"—approve of—me. But love is not the same as approval. Of course I didn't know that back then. I only knew what a phony I was and that I had no clue how to help people. As I've grown to know Christ and his love, he's peeled back the layers of my masks and shown me how being a poser is not necessary. Thank goodness he is able to work through even an imposter like me to help others and change lives.

When I first started in the career world, I was determined to make my mark as a successful career woman. I fell into all the traps of marketing myself as an aggressive woman, independent and self-reliant, even though as a child I was very shy. I was sensitive and tender-hearted as a girl, with hardly an opinion to express. But in the deeply set pattern of wearing whichever mask would help me succeed, I lost sight of the woman God created. Fresh out of graduate school, instead of following my childhood dream to enter into the counselling field I chose instead the business world of consulting, where I could make my mark with a lot of money and influence top business organizations.

But then, coming back into the Christian world, I learned that a "godly" woman is gentle and submissive and only quotes Bible passages when she speaks. She gladly cooks meals for 100 guests at a moment's notice, then lovingly and willingly submits to her husband's needs after she has cleaned up after the guests and left the house spotless. She raises 15 kids without *ever* losing her temper, and all her kids grow up to be pastors and missionaries who credit her with their salvation and perfect Christian lives. That began a quest to take on the mask of a "godly Christian woman," which led to even more loss of the true me and the shutting down of my voice—something I struggle with to this day. I learned to push down any signs of anger or aggression and beat myself down if I felt too strident or asserted opposition.

As I've grown in my work, I've realized how little I know. I don't need all the right answers, and life isn't about becoming lovable but about being loved and being loving toward others. In fact, as I've been able to acknowledge to God that I don't have the answers to help people, he has been able to work through me much more effectively, without the constant static and interference of my old way. I used to see Isaiah 61 as a prescription for how we're to help others:

To bring good news to the poor…to comfort the brokenhearted and to proclaim that captives will be released and prisoners will be freed. He has sent me to tell those who mourn that…he will give a crown of beauty for ashes, a joyous blessing instead of mourning. (Isaiah 61:1–3, NLT)

I *loved* those words when I first read them, but because my work was coming out of a spirit of performance, it grew to become a yoke around me, a sense of pressure to always be "on" and to be responsible to help others.

The more "successful" I became, the more people put me on a pedestal, and the harder I had to work to meet their expectations. Then I realized that in my own self-centred need I had allowed others to put me on that pedestal—I had hungrily clawed onto that in my own neediness and addiction for approval. And so I had set myself up to be their "saviour," causing them to expect more and more from me. I could no longer blame others for their demands on me; I could no longer whine about how everyone wanted a piece of me—I had set myself up to live upon that endlessly spinning carousel.

A Mask for Every Occasion

During a time of utter weariness, serving in six different ministries (yes, it's true), moving very quickly to burnout, I grew short-tempered and unable to cope with the challenges of two busy little kids. God led me to another book that helped to transform me called *Posers, Fakers and Wannabes* by Brennan Manning and Jim Hancock. Some of their words cut to the core:

I'm a Poser too…I have a mask for every occasion. At my worst, I'm not much more than a mirror held up so people see a faint reflection of themselves when they look at me. I hope they like what they see. That is, of course, why I do it: to be liked. The Poser in me trembles at the thought of disappointing people. Fear makes him incapable of direct speech. He hedges, waffles, procrastinates. The Poser is scared silent by the threat of rejection. My fake self protects me…If I do good, I am good. If that fails, the Poser settles for looking good: it's not whether you win or lose, it's how you look playing the game. Look amazing, feel amazing.[13]

As I read further, their words continued to pierce:

Posers are frantic for approval. We have an almost suffocating need to please, which makes it difficult to say *no*, even when *no* is the right answer. Posers are habitually overcommitted…with the fear of not living up to expectations…Posers bury or disguise our true feelings to get what we want. Which makes emotional honesty impossible.[14]

And even more alarmingly,

It gets worse. We even withhold our true selves from God—and then wonder why we're not feeling the love. It's a crazy strategy that can only hurt us because we were made for intimacy with God. Whatever we do to interrupt that just makes us feel less human, less like ourselves. We are made for God, and nothing less will satisfy us.[15]

Reading that felt like a giant kick to my gut. But at the same time, it was also a deep encouragement. It led me to start a journey that was so freeing. I realized I would never discover my true identity as God's daughter unless I began identifying and laying down my masks. And so I began a process of stripping away the defences I had built up over the years. Maybe if I meet with God as the real *me*, the wall around my heart could begin to come down.

Goodbye, Poser

In *Posers, Fakers and Wannabes*, the authors challenge us to write a letter to our posers inside, expressing our true feelings to them—our fears and insecurities, the purpose they served in our lives and why we needed them. This was difficult. Even more difficult, they challenged me to share the letter with close friends, to truly let down my guard with them. But with fear and trembling, I did it. And afterwards, I had never felt so good.

Although I was close to the friends I shared my letter with in that we "did life" together, we had never really gotten that vulnerable with each other before. It's not something any of us were particularly comfortable with. So when I suggested we do this exercise as a group, there were varying degrees of resistance. And part of me wondered if I was laying the groundwork for a public humiliation— you know the kind, where everyone listens uncomfortably, laughs nervously, and then pretends you never ripped open your heart to them. But somehow everyone agreed, and we did it one night in the dining room of one of my friends' homes. Although some of us entered into this exercise less openly than others, I didn't judge them for that; it was where they were at the time, and I was just grateful for their willingness to try. This was a pivotal time in our friendship as it began to move us to a place of greater authenticity. Today, these are my lifelong friends.

As for me, when I read my letter out loud, I wept publicly for the first time with this group of friends, after wearing a mask of self-control for years. I felt so exposed after I read that letter to them, but as they responded with love and understanding, my journey began towards discovering my true identity, not in what I do or who I can convince but who I truly *am*—warts and all.

Dropping my masks and fears allowed me to let go of the pressure I felt from others' expectations as well. And out of that grew freedom to be known and loved by God in a deeper way than I ever thought possible. I began to understand how I could go to him without earning it, my raw, true self, and receive his complete acceptance, grace and love just as I am, for who he made in me, though flawed and sinful as I am. I began to accept how beloved and treasured I am. In experiencing his love both directly and through circumstances, worship, nature and godly friends, I learned that God *does* really know me—the total me, that he already foreknew all of my sins, my bad choices, my failures before I was even conceived, and that upon that basis, God chose to put his hand on my life and make me a beloved and chosen daughter of his.

I also began to realize that in God's eyes, my life isn't defined by what *I do*. He doesn't view me based on my sin struggles or my failures as a Christian; actually, as he looks at me, he sees me as holy and blameless because of Jesus Christ in me (Ephesians 1:4). I can trust my loving Father, who knows all about me yet still chooses to place his love upon me. He has seen me at my ugliest, yet he still loves me. As Manning and Hancock say, "Accepting the reality of my brokenness means accepting my authentic self."[16]

Digging Deep

What's stirring in your soul as you read this? Are you longing to drop your masks and stop faking it? Think about all the times in your life when you felt you had to be "on," when you couldn't be honest with how you really felt, when you chose to pretend to be someone you weren't. What's the cause of that?

If you don't know whether you wear masks, consider these questions: If I were to ask you to describe yourself, could you talk about your strengths and weaknesses with confidence? In other words, do you know who you really are? Are you always the same in how you act regardless of the situation you're in? When you are around others, do you ever feel strained and uncomfortable and find it hard to relax? Has anyone ever told you that they thought you were one way but then when they got to know you better, realized you were another way? Has anyone ever commented on how you act differently around various people? Do you ever act like you don't care what others think, but deep down it really stings when others judge or reject you? Do you ever try to act like something doesn't bother you, but really you're feeling hurt? Do you ever pretend to like someone you really don't?

What might some of your masks be? The *I've-got-it-all-together* mask? The *I'm-a-victim* mask? The *I'm-a-good-Christian* mask? Think about different situations in your life—work, school, church, home, with friends, with family, etc.— what mask might emerge during those times?

Take some time now to write a letter to *your* poser and let it really know what you feel. Make sure you think about when it came around and what purposes it served for you. And then pray for God to provide the courage to share your letter with some close friends. Don't worry about how they will respond— they may not be in the place where they're willing to go deep with you, and so their support and understanding may not be what you want. That's okay, as that's their journey, and it can't be forced. But do it more for your own step of faith, and leave the rest to God.

CHAPTER 9

What's Wrong with Me?

"If I am guilty—woe to me! Even if I am inno-
cent, I cannot lift my head, for I am full of shame
and drowned in my affliction."

Job 10:15

June kept her head down as she spoke, unable to look me in the eye as she finally told me her most shameful secret. Even 20 years after the deed, she could not let go of the guilt and shame she carried around like a millstone. The tears came rolling down her cheeks as she spoke, the pain as fresh as the day she made the decision to abort her baby.

Even though she had been very sick at the time—near death—and had followed the advice of her doctors and her husband, she still could not forgive herself for having murdered her own child. Even though she had gone on to bear four more children, she could not forget the one she had left behind in a small grave, marked only by a tiny cross.

As I listened to June's story, my heart hurt for her—not only for the loss of her child but for the 20 lost years of her life, given over to the unrelentingly cruel taskmaster of shame. She experienced little joy or freedom with the many good gifts God had given her—including a loving husband and four wonderful children—as she regularly flogged herself for her "unforgivable" sin. She overcompensated by trying to be the perfect wife and mother, ignoring her own health and well-being to meet their needs and even their simple wants. And so she had come to my office, suffering from persistent anxiety that had become more and more debilitating. Her conscience was so hyperactive that she repeatedly recounted every mistake she made in a day, which drove her to greater perfectionism and anxiety, leading to unexplained pain and insomnia.

What's Wrong with Me?

The age-old battle with shame is compounded many times over by the fact that it isolates us, makes us hide and keeps us hidden, also preventing us from healing through reaching out to others and God. It convinces us we're alone and should stay there; no one would ever understand the darkness in our hearts. "If they *really* knew me…"

From the work in my counselling office and my personal experience, I believe there is no more devastating bondage than shame. Shame isn't just from the awful feelings of failure because of sins but also from the negative messages we receive as children, which are often compounded as adults. Growing up through abuse, abandonment, rejection and others' failures, we come to believe there is something *wrong* with us, that we aren't lovable, that it's somehow always our fault, because *we* are the common denominator, the deeply flawed cause.

From the Garden of Eden until today, men and women have struggled with shame. Imagine with me how Adam and Eve must have felt as they were forced to leave the garden and faced the consequences of their sin. Imagine the intense shame that must have gripped them as they faced a life without their God to protect and guide them because they had messed up *so* badly. I can just hear them beating themselves up: *We had everything yet we still messed up—what's wrong with us?*

And yet, God in his grace didn't let go of them, and even in the midst of all that he allowed them to suffer as they began life out of the Garden of Eden, he still was with them. How he must have longed to comfort them as they struggled with beginning life in the harsh world outside of Eden. I wonder if Adam or Eve ever reached out to the Lord or if they chose to bear their pain on their own. We aren't told of how they were able to bear up under the pain of a life afflicted with sin, shame and pain, but their story of suffering is the same as it is for us today.

Legitimate Versus Illegitimate Shame

Before we go on, it's important to distinguish between *legitimate* and *illegitimate* shame. Legitimate shame—guilt or conviction—is a deep sense of our failure before a perfect God. We *know* we are guilty, and that moves us to confess with a contrite heart. Illegitimate shame is an identity issue attacking your God-given personhood—your very *being*, not based in the things you've done but who you are. Legitimate shame is guilt for *what* you do, whereas illegitimate shame is believing you are bad for *who* you are.

"Godly sorrow brings repentance that leads to salvation and leaves no regret, but worldly sorrow brings death" (2 Corinthians 7:10). Worldly sorrow—or illegitimate shame—leads to despair, which leads to condemnation, which leads to self-abasement. There is no freedom from sin, and in fact, you're stuck in a repeat cycle of sin and shame. You feel worthless, that you are bad and therefore without hope, since your shame becomes a part of *who* you are. You feel you're flawed, worthless, discarded, so you need to hide who you are.

But hiding in shame keeps us from being known, from receiving the grace of God. Shame feels so bad that we must work to earn others' and God's love. Wrong behaviour can be confessed and forgiven. But illegitimate shame is a root problem, hidden below the surface, that bears the fruit of self-contempt. Because shame is so painful to experience, many of us bury our feelings about it rather than letting the pain point us to a sickness that needs medicine.

Years ago, psychiatrist Carl Jung said of the human condition,

The acceptance of oneself is the essence of the whole moral problem and the epitome of a whole outlook on life. That I feed the hungry, that I forgive an insult, that I love my enemy in the name of Christ—all these are undoubtedly great virtues. What I do unto the least of my brethren, that I do unto Christ. But what if I should discover that the least amongst them all, the poorest of the beggars, the most impudent of the offenders, the very enemy himself—that these are within me, and that I myself stand in need of the alms of my own kindness—that I myself am the enemy who must be loved—what then? As a rule, the Christian's attitude is then reversed: there is no longer any question of love or long-suffering; we say to the brother within us, "Raca," and condemn and rage against ourselves. We hide it from the world; we refuse to admit ever having met the least among the lowly in ourselves.[17]

Raca—meaning "empty-headed" or "fool"—is a word of utter scorn and contempt. Self-contempt, self-criticism, self-judgment and self-hatred are all rooted in intense shame and a sense of unworthiness and rejection of ourselves.

Does this sound familiar? Do you regularly beat yourself up ferociously even while you extend grace and mercy towards others? Do you readily accept negative words of dismissal and criticism from others but reject and ignore words of positive affirmation and encouragement? Or has your shame so consumed you that you no longer can even understand grace—either for yourself or others—and are filled with bitter cynicism and rejection of others?

A deep sorrow for me when I counsel people is when I witness their deep shame and feelings of self-condemnation that keep them trapped in a prison of misery. I was that way once, and that was a very dark time. Satan still tries to tempt me to go back there, particularly when I'm confronted with the reality of my sinful heart. But God's grace is so abundant that as I hold on to the truth of his grace, he is able to woo me back to him to receive my Father's unconditional love and to rest in him.

Secret Shame

When the Lord first began to bring me back to him after my extended time of rebellion over a decade, I started to grow in my head knowledge of what it was to be a follower of Jesus Christ. I began attending church again and reading my Bible. And as I grew in my knowledge of God, I began to try to practice "godly" behaviours and get involved in the Christian community. But deep within my heart, I carried a very secret shame, terrified someone would discover how bad I really was and the sinful choices I had made. I was in such bondage to my secret shame that I had nightmares of being discovered, and I wrestled many hours in a repetitive cycle of reliving my shameful choices.

To make things worse, my work as a Christian counsellor and my ministries were taking off, and many people were receiving care and relief from their own burdens. I was being asked to speak at conferences and retreats, and my circle of influence kept growing. I felt them placing me on a pedestal, which only made the fear and shame grow greater.

I understood God's forgiveness and grace at an intellectual level, but I could not receive that into my heart. This shame was so large that I literally could not feel God's love. I was so focused on the shame that I could not consider what the cross and grace really meant. The shame drove me harder to practice good works and become "godly," in the hopes that I could bury that shameful part of me with good works.

It didn't work. Instead, it led to beating myself up every time I sinned and to more effort to resist sin in my life, and of course I'd fail and heap on more condemnation. I was stuck in a quagmire of shame and secrets from which I could see no way out. It robbed me of any joy in my relationship with the Lord. And I was certainly not experiencing the full life.

And then one restless night, out of desperation, I cried out to the Lord for release from this shame. I wrestled with him as he coaxed me to surrender it to him. But it would take a huge leap of faith. He told me that I needed to bring my dark secrets out to light, which terrified me. With his gentle and patient guidance, he gave me the courage to take that leap.

He led me to confessing all of my past to my mentor, Adrienne, a very godly and loving woman, who simply embraced me and was grace embodied to me. As she tenderly held my face between her hands and looked into my eyes with love, she began to speak God's words of love and forgiveness and grace to me. Not once was there condemnation or judgment in her eyes. As I began to experience her love washing over me, I felt for the first time God's grace washing over me. She didn't say anything I didn't already know in my head, what I knew God had said, but through her words spoken to me, I finally *experienced* grace deeply in my heart.

It was in that context of grace and love that I began to come out of the pit of shame; it was in the truth of God's amazing grace for me that I began to peel back the layers and masks, to seek to be more authentic on this journey of discovering the *real* me. I learned I needed to allow God to define me—not my sins or my failures but my identity as his chosen daughter. I also realized I needed to let God and others pursue me in my shame. God covers us with garments of what he's sacrificed and offers us grace to clothe us with dignity so we won't feel ashamed.

And out of that freedom from shame, I was able to offer the same grace to June. As we met week after week, she was able to work through a process of self-forgiveness and embrace fully the truth of God's grace for her. Because I was able to be grace to her—listening to her story session after session without judgment—and help her see herself as a beloved child of God, June began to heal.

Out of the pit of my shame came grace, and from that, freedom for others, a hundredfold. Can you see the hand of God all over my story? Can you begin to see the same for yours?

God Is Pursuing You

If you allow him to, God will enter your shame and pursue you to love you, forgive you, clothe you in dignity and restore in you an awareness of who you really are in Christ. He will also bring people into your life who will see the real you and love you anyway, the people who will enter your shame with you and offer you grace—maybe some of the people in your life right now that he may even be bringing to mind.

Do you know that when God sees you now, he sees you as holy and blameless, clothed in righteousness because of Jesus in you? No matter how much you fail, no matter how many times you fall and sin, no matter how many times you mess up—*nothing* will ever take away from you the love of God. But you have to open yourself up to true love, because true love heals, true love knows who you are and sees everything about you. That means coming before the Lord naked and honest, laying it all down before him. Not because he doesn't already know but because *you* need to experience his love and grace in the face of your shame and brokenness. Counterfeit love, on the other hand, is based on your masks, what you can do for others, how holy you can try to be. There is no power to heal in counterfeit love.

Do You Love Me?

I was reading through John 21 during a recent spiritual retreat, pondering the passage where Jesus comes back to meet with his disciples after his crucifixion. During that encounter, Jesus has a dialogue with Peter, who had just betrayed him three times. He asks Peter three times, "Do you love me?" and then after Peter says yes, he says, "Then take care of my sheep." I had always focused on that part, "take care of my sheep," as Jesus calling *me* to care for his people. But Jesus never asks Peter about his denial or even makes any comment about or rebukes him for his betrayal. Jesus makes absolutely no mention of Peter's sin but instead focuses on Peter's *heart:* Do you love me? Jesus isn't focusing on Peter's sin; Jesus is nailing Peter's *desire,* his heart. And I have no doubt that Peter loved Jesus and wanted to fully live for him.

That really struck me—my heart's longing is to live for Christ. Although I continue to mess up and deny Jesus, he knows all about my sins yet embraces me and loves others through me. He sees my heart's desire, and he is pleased and wants to *use* me, even as messed up as I am.

We get so hung up on our performance, beating ourselves up when we sin or mess up, while Jesus just wants us to love him and to love others. When we're so focused on our sin and messing up, we turn inwards, and it becomes about us rather than about the Lord. We end up taking our eyes off of him, and when that happens, it's certain we'll fall flat on our faces. Our messed-up lives are the fruit of not merely our sins but our inability to trust the Lord and know deeply how his love and grace heals us. If we don't know his love and grace for us, we can't trust him fully, and if we don't trust him fully, we can't fully surrender to him and break free from shame.

Listen to God's declarations to you through Brennan Manning's words in *Abba's Child:*

God calls us to stop hiding and come openly to him. God is the father who ran to his prodigal son when he came limping home. God weeps over us when shame and self-hatred immobilizes us. Yet as soon as we lose our nerve about ourselves, we take cover. Adam and Eve hid, and we all, in one way or another, have used them as role models...But God loves who we really are—whether we like it or not. God calls us, as he did Adam, to come out of hiding. No amount of spiritual makeup can render us more presentable to him...His love, which called us into existence, calls us to come out of self-hatred and step into his truth. "Come to me *now*," Jesus says. "Acknowledge and accept who I want to be for you: a Savior of boundless compassion, infinite patience, unbearable forgiveness, and love that keeps no score of wrongs. Quit projecting onto Me your own feelings about yourself. At this moment your life is a bruised reed and I will not crush it, a smoldering wick and I will not quench it. *You are in a safe place.*"[18]

Digging Deep

So what does God want to say to you right now? How does your heart respond to his invitation through Brennan Manning's words? Will you choose to invite God into your shame and allow his grace and love to bring healing in your life? Choose now to lay your shame before him, lay before your Father all that you have kept hidden in the dark.

Are you ready? Take some time now to pray:

Lord, I confess that I have not lived out of the freedom of the cross of Jesus Christ. Instead, I have allowed my feelings of shame to keep me in bondage to self-criticism, self-hatred and self-punishment. Please forgive me for my failure to receive your grace and my attempts to earn my forgiveness. I choose now to receive your gift of forgiveness.

Holy Spirit, reveal to me now all the ways that I have not allowed the forgiveness of Jesus Christ to release me.

I place before me now a big box [picture in your mind whatever box or bag you want to use to get rid of all your shame—be creative with what works for you; it could be a garbage dump, steel box, or a garbage bag], and I place in it the following ways that I have not accepted your forgiveness. Lord, I choose to forgive myself for _____ [list everything that God brings to mind].

When they are all in the box, seal it shut (lock it if you'd like!) and give the whole thing to Jesus. Picture him taking it all away from you.

I now give up the right to punish myself, and I choose to release myself from the prison of guilt that I have made for myself. I accept myself as forgiven. Lord, please take away the pain that I have brought upon myself, so that I may be free to love myself and love others. I pray this in the precious name of Jesus Christ. Amen.

Now here's the tough next step: Ask the Lord to bring to mind someone—a godly friend, mentor, pastor or counsellor—to whom you can confess all of your secrets, not to receive absolution but to *experience* your Father's grace for you. And go do it. Freedom from shame is waiting for you.

CHAPTER 10

Is My Life a Lie?

The poor, deluded fool feeds on ashes. He trusts something that can't help him at all. Yet he cannot bring himself to ask, "Is this idol that I'm holding in my hand a lie?"

Isaiah 44:20, NLT

Justin paced angrily back and forth in my office. His arms waved aggressively as he talked, so furious that he could not sit still. He was fuming at the actions of his boss, which he saw as a direct betrayal of him and a complete disrespect for his ideas and his leadership of his team.

"What does he know?" he shouted in fury. "How dare he override my authority with my team? How could he disagree with my ideas, and even worse, do it in front of *my* people? Does he think I'm an idiot? Well, if he can't see the value I bring to the team, then I'm done!"

Justin described how he had gone "toe to toe" with his boss, enraged by his actions, how he "let him have it." Even now he could not contain his anger as he relived the encounter in excruciating detail, the emotional turmoil as fresh as if he were there. I let Justin vent, knowing he needed to process his anger, but when his emotions were clearly escalating, I interrupted him and spoke gently.

"Justin, what do you think is going on for you? I wonder if there's more going on here than just feeling angry about what your boss has done."

At first, he continued to sputter on, unable to see past his rage. I went on speaking softly and compassionately. "If I were in your shoes, I would probably be feeling much the same—disrespected and unvalued. I can understand how hard you work, and then to be treated like that in front of your team—it probably would have made anyone feel worthless, like they didn't matter."

At my words, Justin suddenly became quiet, his anger deflating just as quickly as it had exploded. He began to nod, eyes reddening as he fought to control his emotions. For a very brief moment, Justin looked as vulnerable as a little boy trying to hold back his tears after being bullied in the playground, but then just as quickly he pulled himself back together and resumed his mask of neutrality, a wall going up as high as a fort's barricade to keep everyone out. He took a deep breath and then began to look embarrassed about his loss of control, his temporary vulnerability.

Undeterred, I continued to gently push him to enter into the truth of his heart's pain, to get to the bottom of what was really going on for him. I knew that freedom for Justin would come only if he allowed himself to experience his pain enough to grieve and heal. Only then would he begin to understand and let go of the many ways he used to shore up his shaky sense of worth—all the ways that kept people away from truly loving him and prevented him from receiving God's love. While he'd convinced himself this was the "safest" way to manage life and relationships he'd found to be so untrustworthy, Justin didn't understand that it also kept him locked in his destructive patterns that ultimately only caused him more pain and isolation.

Justin had been raised by a harsh and cold father who didn't know how to love him properly, who was critical and demanding, who inadvertently communicated to Justin that his value was in his performance and achievement. He was also raised by a weak and passive mother who allowed his father to bully him and who dealt with her own pain by avoidance and trying to placate his angry dad. Not only did this create in Justin a pattern of handling his own hurts and disappointments with anger, but it led to a false image of love, an idol to which he clung.

Out of that false image of love, Justin constructed certain rules about what love ought to look like: he began to believe that if someone disagreed with him or didn't like one of his ideas, that person was automatically against him, and he or she became an adversary who needed to be rejected (before that person rejected him). He also believed that if someone was critical of him or appeared to dismiss him, that person was out to get him and had to be cut off from his life. He began to crave the adulation and praise of others, and he could not get enough affirmation or approval from them. As he began to lead more team members in his climb up the corporate ladder, he liked to surround himself with people who flattered him and put him on a pedestal, who were willing to follow him regardless of what he said or did. He could not tolerate anything less. His deep inadequacy was too uncomfortable to bear.

DR. MERRY C. LIN

Counterfeit Love

As difficult as Justin was to love because of his angry and aggressive ways, I felt compassion for him. You see, I too have clung for years to my own false image of love, believing that I would only be loved if I bent over backward to accommodate others and make them happy. It meant putting my own needs and desires aside to do what I thought it took to gain acceptance. It was only after coming to the end of my ability to keep up my frenetic lifestyle that I finally began to see how I had replaced my God-given need to be accepted with an idol.

Anthony DeMello says it disconcertingly well in *The Way to Love:*

Look at your life and see how you have filled its emptiness with people. As a result they have a stranglehold on you. See how they control your behavior by their approval and disapproval. They hold the power to ease your loneliness with their company, to send your spirits soaring with their praise, to bring you down to the depths with their criticism and rejection. Take a look at yourself spending almost every waking moment of your day placating and pleasing people, whether they are living or dead. You live by their norms, conform to their standards, seek their company, desire their love, dread their ridicule, long for their applause, meekly submit to the guilt they lay upon you; you are terrified to go against the fashion in the way you dress or speak or act or even think.[19]

Ouch!

A few years ago, I was wrestling with shame, recognizing the patterns of falsehoods and masks I hid behind, even with my closest friends and family. Because of my deep fear of disappointing others and my lust for their approval, I struggled to be honest with them about my feelings, particularly my anger, and I knew I would sometimes "act out" loving deeds without a genuine desire or motivation to love. I avoided conflict at all costs, and when I was hurt or angered, I would typically isolate myself to lick my wounds.

I had the respect of many, but I knew that much of their positive regard was built on the shaky foundation of my efforts. I knew I was all too often motivated by fear of disapproval rather than by godly love, and I recognized how often I chased the temporary high of the approval of others to avoid feeling the emptiness within me. This hunger for approval led to patterns of deception so subtle I deceived even myself about it.

My ability to lie to myself came crashing down during my season of burnout, when I was too exhausted to keep up the pretense any longer. Picture this: I had gotten to the point where I was hiding from everyone, even friends and family, because I could no longer fake it. Being around people meant performing. At the height of my depression, I withdrew completely and went to spend some time alone in my little trailer tucked in the woods. Fearful of anyone knowing I was there, I kept the shades closed all day and folded down the awning so that it blocked the doorway and two-thirds of my trailer, like an abandoned house with boarded-up windows warning "Don't come near."

I was so tired of performing that I finally had to face my sinful patterns of hiddenness. But what could I do instead? It was all I knew to do. I wept, hopeless of ever breaking free of my lies, afraid of being rejected if I got honest with my friends and family. Desperate, I cried out to God and asked him to show me what was going on. He lovingly revealed the lies I believed, things like "I can never break free, I'm doomed. It's hopeless to change. It's all up to me and I can't do it. I'm a fraud and a fake. I'm bad." He then began to whisper truths to me: "The truth will set you free. I will change you. It's not up to you, I will help you. You can do all things through Christ who gives you strength. You are redeemed. You are holy and blameless in my eyes because of Jesus in you."

He then revealed to me the source of these lies, showing me the patterns of isolation and abandonment I experienced as a young child, growing up with parents who were too busy and overwhelmed with the stress of the loss of their son. He showed me how I withdrew into a fantasy world to cope with the loneliness and pain, reinforcing the isolation and distrust I had for others' love: how I believed no one would ever truly be there for me, that it was too risky to open up my heart fully, because in the end, no one would care, that if I wanted anything, it was all up to me. Out of that wound grew the fruit of performing, hiding and deceiving—all to protect my heart from what I feared most, abandonment.

I then asked the Lord, "What truth will set me free? I long to be free." And he replied, "True love—to receive and to give. True love heals." And that's when it hit me: I wasn't giving anyone in my life a chance to really love me—the true, hurting, vulnerable, struggling me. Because of my fears, I was chasing counterfeit love. I was trying to give others an image, for fear that they wouldn't love the real me. I realized I had to lay down this idol to allow God to do his work of healing. As long as I continued to reach for the counterfeit, he couldn't bring true love to heal my life. And for God to heal me as he wanted to, I had to let go of the counterfeit love to which I was clinging. I also began to realize that God didn't condemn me for my sinful patterns of hiding. Instead, he felt such sorrow for me. As I sat with him and wept in my pain, I sensed his heart aching for me and that it always had as he watched my struggle.

It was then that I finally understood what God wanted—that I wasn't meant to waste my pain by running away from facing it. God's heart hurt for me in my suffering, but even so, he wanted me to enter into my pain to receive healing and freedom, to receive true love—the true love that heals.

True Love Heals

That was a turning point in *all* my relationships. That was when I began to open up, even as I began to let go of the counterfeit love and my idol of others' approval. That was when my eyes were finally open to all the idols in my life, all the ways I had given away what rightfully belonged to God.

A few days after my time of grieving with the Lord, I asked him to search my heart and show me anything not pleasing to him, and he revealed my fear, control, manipulation, perfectionism, people pleasing, pride, worry about what others thought, unbelief, unloving actions and thoughts, selfishness, and demanding my own way. When my eyes were opened to the truth of the idolatry in my life, I finally saw the stronghold it had claimed. I saw all the ways it held me back from the life God meant me to live and how it robbed me of joy and peace. And finally, I allowed the Lord to purge the idols from my life.

When Justin also chose to face the idols in his life—the false ways he received love and affirmation—he began to open himself up to true love. It wasn't easy, because he had to let go of his "rules" of how others should act if they loved him. He had to turn away from his old thinking that put all sorts of conditions on how others should treat him. This was hard work for Justin, and he experienced many setbacks because of his negative interpretations of others when they failed to meet those conditions.

As he began to open up to me, his growing vulnerability scared him. The more he allowed himself to value our relationship, the bigger the risk of possible loss. And so when I confronted him, he took offence, believing that I was now against him. When I disappointed him, he was deeply hurt, thinking I no longer cared for him. He picked through all of my words obsessively, looking for evidence that I thought ill of him or was rejecting him.

Many times, he wanted to walk away. It was too painful to face his vulnerabilities, his desperate need for love and affirmation. Far easier to go back to his old ways, when he pretended he didn't care and used his anger to keep people away from his hurting self. But over time, with what he experienced in my office—grace balanced by truth, care protected by boundaries, compassion balanced with conviction—he began to form a healthy attachment and a resilience to handle the normal ups and downs of relationships. And out of that, he began to receive true love from his Father.

We were created to feast on God, who *is* love, to be completely filled by him. But if we don't seek him out, a vacuum is created in our hearts, a disaster in the making. If we aren't filled with him, we default to being needy people seeking to be filled by others or resorting to using substances to gain fulfillment or temporary highs and numbness from pain. All these things can quickly gain a power in our lives and ultimately destroy us. Even the most perfect human love cannot satisfy us: "*My soul finds rest in God*" (Psalm 62:1).

Digging Deep

Does Justin's story resonate with you at all? Or my story? Do you find yourself secretly longing for acceptance, affirmation and love? What about *your* "rules" for love?

Do you have a craving for anything? This can be a good thing—such as enjoying others and revelling in the good gifts that God gives you. But where it eventually becomes a betrayer is if these things take the place of God in your life and become your only source of joy and satisfaction. These good things can become a bondage if you haven't let God fill you.

What is God stirring in your heart as you read this chapter? Ask God this honest question: "Search my heart, O God, and reveal to me anything that's not pleasing to you." Are there any addictions or idols that the Lord is bringing to your mind? If there's anything you know has a stronghold and you're having difficulty breaking free, do yourself a favour and reach out for help from a trustworthy source; a Christian counsellor, therapist or psychologist could offer compassionate solutions.

Reflect on the pain in your life right now. What are you doing with it? Have you been running away from it? Have you been relying on something other than God to relieve it? What does it reveal? What might God be up to? How might he redeem it? Can you believe your sorrow has a purpose in your life? Remember, don't waste your pain!

SECTION II

Rescuing Our Souls

---

*So then, let us not be like others, who are asleep,
but let us be awake.*

1 Thessalonians 5:6

CHAPTER 11

Death Before Life

Truly, truly, I say to you, unless a grain of wheat
falls into the earth and dies, it remains alone; but
if it dies, it bears much fruit.

John 12:24, NASB

I curled up on the couch, weeping uncontrollably. I—the one always in control—was sobbing like a baby. Great wails convulsed me in a mortifying way I didn't even recognize as my own. Was this really me? Even worse, I really didn't know why or understand what was happening to me. I was completely exhausted and depressed. I had nothing left in me, alone in my misery and deeply ashamed to be such a mess. I could not get a handle on my emotions. My heart was a stone within me, and my spirit felt dead. I had breath, but where was the life?

I lay on the couch wondering, *Is this the life I was meant to live? How did I come to this place of desperation?*

Out of sheer emotional and physical exhaustion, I had finally been forced to take some time off to recuperate, a sabbatical from my labours, because I realized I could not continue on. I was burnt-out and finally accepted the truth that I was of no good to anyone in the state I was in, just sleepwalking through my life. The many sleepless nights, the numerous mornings I had to drag myself out of bed, the sick feeling in the pit of my stomach every day I drove to work, the inability to think clearly, and the dead feeling in my heart as I listened to another sad story—all of these symptoms pointed to a life out of control.

It was a scary decision to make because of all the people I would be letting down. And frankly, I didn't really know how to stop, since taking time off to *rest* was not something I had done since I started working at the age of 13. Growing up in an immigrant home where financial struggle was the norm, I learned to work hard and push forward regardless of how I felt. I learned to put aside what

I wanted to do in order to help out with the family expenses. People were counting on me; it was just the way it was.

So as I anticipated some upcoming time of rest and quiet during my sabbatical, I was stunned when I almost immediately crashed in total exhaustion and emotional chaos. My usual stoicism and numbness no longer shielded me from the uncomfortable truth: I was going to have to stay still long enough to see what had been going on inside me for years. And I knew that if I did, I would come face to face with the emptiness that was engulfing my soul.

The ironic thing is that when I read my journal entries from years past, the warning signs were there—indications of weariness, joylessness and dryness in my spirit. I tried to manage them by chiding myself for my "wrong attitude."

But now grief came crashing in as I let go of my pretenses and stopped trying to be strong—grief for the years I had lost and for the overwhelming futility of all my efforts.

As I sought to understand why I felt such heaviness in my soul, a picture came to my mind of a barren field in winter, abandoned after being plundered by its users' demands—that was the state of my soul. And the grief swelled. After years of sacrificing and doing what I thought God wanted me to do, this was what I had to show for it. Absolutely nothing. Used and thrown aside! And for what purpose? Was there *any* fruit for all my endless labour?

I didn't know it then, but I realize now that God was unearthing the brokenness in my heart to bring healing into my life. He was allowing me to come to the end of myself and face the emptiness of my own efforts to meet my own needs for value, acceptance and love. He wanted me to stop pretending, stop trying to earn love, and begin to see my value in his eyes.

Let Old Things Die

Into the bleakness of my grief, a small voice whispered hope to me:

"My daughter, you must let go and let old things die so that I can bring new life to you. You must stop fighting me. Your soul is in winter right now but it is for my purposes. Slow down, rest in me, face your pain head-on—and do it with me. I am with you. I know your pain, I weep with you, and I am gentle with your heart. Strip off your efforts and idol of human approval which only produces death—I say this not to condemn you but to free you! Your field is not abandoned and forgotten; it is merely fallow, at rest and recuperating after being overused. Allow the nutrients of my love and grace to soak deep into the thirsty soil of your heart. I promise you, my child, new life will burst forth in great abundance!"

John Eldredge says in *Walking with God,*

God must from time to time, and sometimes very insistently, disrupt our lives *so that* we release our grasping of life here and now. Usually through pain. God is asking us to let go of the things we love and have given our hearts to, so that we can give our hearts even more fully to him. He thwarts us in our attempts to make life work so that our efforts fail, and we must face the fact that we don't really look to God for life. Our first reaction is usually to get angry with him, which only serves to make the point. Don't you hear people say, "Why did God let this happen?" far more than you hear them say, "Why aren't I more fully given over to God?" We see God as a means to an end rather than the end itself. God as the assistant to our life versus God *as* our life. We don't see the process of our life as coming to the place where we are fully his and he is our all.[20]

His thoughts are echoed by Os Hillman:

The Bible often speaks of death as a requirement of living a life in Christ. This death is not a physical death, but a spiritual death. It is a death of the old so the new can be raised. It is the life of Christ that is raised in us. However, this death can be painful if we do not choose to willingly allow this "circumcision of heart" to have its way. If we are not circumcised of heart, we do not enter into God's promises...None of us will ever enter the Promised Land of full blessing with God unless we have this same circumcision of heart.[21]

During my soul's winter, the season of death, I especially took heart from the knowledge that God understands our suffering and is *with* us through the dark times. He allows us—in fact, wants us—to grieve and to lay out our pain before him, to tell him how we *really* feel in our anger and sorrow—so we can finally move on. Grieving the past is a necessary part of moving past death to life; it's necessary to awaken us from our numb state of mere survival through the devastations and disappointments of life. It's a time when we stop ignoring the long-buried feelings of betrayal and abandonment over God letting us down and not being there for us when we most desperately needed him.

The Work of Winter

Mark Buchanan, in his book *Spiritual Rhythms,* describes this time:

Winter seems all-consuming and never-ending....Winter hides God. It has power to sever my knowledge *about* God from my experience *of* him, and to hold the two apart, so that my theology and my reality become irreconcilable...Winter is friendless. In it, we experience a terrible, terrifying aloneness...Abandonment. Rejection. Isolation. This is the shape of the soul in winter...Last and worst, winter is death. It is living death. Death haunts us and surrounds those in winter.[22]

He goes on to illustrate the "work" of winter, which requires great fortitude and is hard labour that's needed and restoring in its own way—the work of praying, pruning and waiting, all in preparation for the fruit that is to come in springtime. But deep in the throes of wintertime, I couldn't even begin to imagine the fruit that was too come. I was just trying to survive.

With nothing left in me, I was forced to pray, not because God had been good to me or answered my prayers but because God's Word says he is good and faithful and sovereign. Looking back, I realize that it was an incredible time of faith building, a time of walking by faith and not by sight, a time of clinging to the certainty of things hoped for and the assurance of things unseen (Hebrews 11:1). There is no better soil than wintertime for growing an enduring faith that withstands the worst storms that life can throw at you, even when it feels like God has turned his face away from you.

And the pruning...to be stripped bare—naked, fruitless, ugly—right down to the core of my roots. To have everything revealed in all my unsightly glory. To realize how much deadwood I was holding on to because of my fears of letting go, all of my "responsibilities" and legalistic rules. But as every gardener knows, the harder you prune—if done right—the more luscious and bountiful the fruit will be. Winter then becomes a season when God does some of his best creative, revealing work, a mutilation that's really a cultivation of beauty.

And it's in winter—during the long, hard, cold months—that our roots grow deep and strong. It's when being battered by the harsh storms that our faith takes hold in the deepest ways, becoming unshakable and unmoveable. And when you're forced to wait on God, that's when you're driven to keep believing even in the face of his silence, because you have nothing else to hold on to.

I now see in retrospect how long I was actually in winter, how it crept up on me without me even realizing it. I think it's because it didn't begin with a singular event that marked the season of winter. In fact, winter kind of limped in, and I didn't even really notice how cold I was.

Looking back, I realized how long I fought allowing winter to do its work. I had hung on and told myself I had no choice—it was my responsibility to keep going. And so I tried to fight the pruning that God was doing in my life for my own good, because I couldn't see my way out of my mess of a life.

And God's pruning in my life? He was putting to death many things: my need to prove myself or earn his approval, my need to perform or try to be holy and sacrificial in my own efforts and strength, my belief of him as a demanding and stingy God, and religiosity. All of the things prevented true fruit from growing in my life, fruit through the Holy Spirit rather than through self-effort.

The Gift of Winter

I was beginning to understand the absolute gift God had given me through my winter season, hard as it was to believe there could be anything good about this dark and cold time of my life. But when everything is stripped away—all the false beliefs, idols, and self-sufficiency—and you come before God, naked in your longing and sorrow, you *will* find your rest and strength and sustenance in him. And most freeing for me, a heart in winter is *supposed to* lie dormant so that it can rest and be nurtured. The burden of responsibility lightens in this season, and there comes a release to do things you can only do in winter and to cease doing things that cannot be done in winter. And so, a time to pray, prune and wait on God, and a time to rest.

As I chose to embrace death so that I could live, I decided I needed to have a funeral to mourn my death and a wake to celebrate my ending and new life. Having spent hours journaling about all that God was pruning in me, I decided to write each of my "cancers" on sheets of paper—pride, approval-seeking, self-sufficiency, and so on—and set them on fire. A ritual, to be sure, but there was something so satisfying in cremating my past life.

And then a wake—a time to celebrate my new life. I treated myself to a spa and a great meal out with some good friends. Hoo-rah! And as I began to understand God's purposes in allowing this death in my life, I felt a growing sense of excitement as I contemplated new beginnings, even as I let go of old things. I sensed a breaking free and moving forward.

As I reflected on the hope of new beginnings that arise out of the loss of old ways, I heard Os Hillman's book speaking to my heart:

What we perceive as dark periods in our lives are designed to be treasures from God. They are actually riches stored in secret places. We cannot see those times in this light because of the often-accompanying pain or fear that prevents us from accepting these times as treasures. They have a particular purpose from God's viewpoint: "...so that you may know that I am the Lord...who summons you by name." You see, unless we are cast into times in which we are completely at God's mercy for breakthroughs in our lives, we will never experience God's faithfulness in those areas. We will never know how personal He is, or that He can be trusted to meet the deepest needs in our lives. God wants each of us to know that we are "summoned by name." Every hair of our head is numbered. He knows every activity we are involved in. His love for you and me knows no bounds, and He will take every opportunity to demonstrate this to us.[23]

Digging Deep

Dan Allender captures it well in his book *To Be Told:* "Denouement is an ending that serves as the prelude for a new beginning; there is always the next turn in the road. A new Story begins the moment the old one ends."[24]

Where are you in your story? Are you in a season of winter or dying to old things? Has God brought you into a place of darkness? Trust him today to reveal the hidden treasure that can be found in this darkness. There are times in all of our lives when we must open ourselves to seeking God with all our hearts, times when he brings us to a place of "death" in some aspect of our lives, so that we can pause and pay attention to him. When we recognize that we have no ability in our own strength to change or affect the events around us, we are in position to hear from God. And if you're currently in the winter season, give yourself permission to grieve with God, to walk through the darkness of your pain, so that you can open yourself up to the redemption of your story. Do that, please, I urge you.

Are you hungry for a personal encounter with God? Then take the time to allow him to sweep away the dead things in your life and in your soul. If you're in winter, prune hard. Cut away the dead things in your life, both spiritually and practically. What activities, tasks or relationships are draining the life away from you and producing no fruit? Take a look at all the unhealthy branches of your life—the travel, the committees, the unfinished projects, the obsessions, the sins, the diversions, the proliferation of responsibilities that aren't really yours.

Look at your typical week or your activities over the last month or so. Write down everything you did—or tried to do, all of your tasks, responsibilities and meetings. Ask yourself honestly whether these things are bearing fruit or just sapping energy. Cut away those things that are rooted in your insecurities, fears or idols, anything other than God. Be ruthless in cleaning out the deadwood. Take the time now so that your soul will be renewed and ready to bear the seeds of the new fruit and new life God wants to bear in you.

CHAPTER 12

Taking Him On

O my people, trust in him at all times. Pour out
your heart to him, for God is our refuge.

Psalm 62:8, NLT

I watched the battle taking place on Doris' face as she fought to hold back her tears. I slowed our conversation down to allow her to take deep breaths and calm her tumultuous emotions. "Doris," I said, "it's okay…let it go." Tears began to flow down her cheeks. Her face worked to maintain its composure, wrestling against the flood buffeting her crumbling control.

I sat quietly, knowing the release must happen, avoiding empty words of reassurance commonly offered when witnessing the immensity of someone's anguish. Finally, the dam broke and Doris hunched over on the couch, keening as if her heart was shattering. She covered her face with her hands, ashamed, but unable to hold it in any longer. The pain was too real to mask anymore.

As she began feeling more of her grief, the sounds coming from deep inside her chest were breaking my heart. All I could do was sit with her in her pain, as she faced the loneliness and feelings of abandonment she felt at the hands of her God. Having never experienced unconditional love or warm nurturance from her emotionally distant mother or her harsh father, she was finally confronting the emotional void in her heart that had stunted her ability to receive her heavenly Father's love.

This began the day Doris embarked on her journey of facing the soul-crippling sorrow that had erected and protected the wall around her heart. Having suffered from depression for much of her life, she could not seem to break free from the dark cloud that surrounded her or the loneliness she felt, no matter what she did or how many people tried to help her. It was only when she began to wrestle with God *in* the darkness and *through* her many experiences of abandonment and betrayal that she began to experience his tender, healing love.

Soul Dead

Seems contrary, doesn't it? How can that dark place be where we experience God's love? It seems easier and sounds better to run from the darkness within and distract ourselves from the pain in our souls. And so this is what most of us spend our lifetimes doing.

As Christians, our guilt at secretly harbouring black thoughts and feelings about God and the life he's given us prevents us from breaking down the wall around our hearts that keeps us numb. And so we become soul dead. The busyness of life provides us a modicum of comfort, so we continue to pretend everything is just fine. We nod through sermons, attend church, get a routine and struggle to apply Scripture, all while avoiding any true honesty and intimacy in our relationships. We distract ourselves with temporary pleasures, go shopping, meet friends, make play dates to trade decorating ideas, and fool ourselves into thinking that we're okay.

None of this is bad in and of itself, we say. *This is just life. Anyway, everyone has problems. The past is the past.*

And then God comes a-knocking on the doors to our hearts. And for many of us, this comes in unexpected and unwelcome packages—things that stop everything and throw a wrench into the routine of life. *That wasn't supposed to happen,* we say. Do we keep pretending we're okay as the mess of our lives gets messier? Do we murmur platitudes, pray more, and deny and defend rather than face the blow to our belief that God is good and loving?

We see people wrestling with God all through Scripture, from David running for his life from his beloved king to Job literally losing everything and even to Jesus on the cross: "*My God, my God, why have you forsaken me?*" (Matthew 27:46).

These are our primary examples of godliness, and all of them felt *betrayed by God.* And yet, each of them made the choice to wrestle with God in gut-honesty. They didn't sin in pouring out their hearts to him in their anger and deep sorrow. Anger at injustice is not a sin. "*In your anger do not sin*" (Ephesians 4:26). Godly people get angry. But out of that wrestling, instead of easy answers, the freedom they experienced cleansed and comforted their hearts and gave assurance that their suffering would be redeemed. And that tenderized their hearts to receive God's love and peace. Out of our experiences of wrestling with God can grow a passion and gratitude for his unfailing love and a life on fire for him.

Isn't that what we really want and what we were all created to have?

How Long, Lord, How Long?

In our buttoned-down, overly-controlled Christian world, we are often loath to create ripples in the stagnant waters of our lives. Not only that, we are so afraid of what would happen if we were to let loose our wails to the heavens that we choose instead to lead an insipid life ruled by "shoulds" and empty performance. That is not God's design for our lives. We will *never* cross the divide between our heads and our hearts and between the truth of Scripture and the experience of that truth in our lives unless we are willing to come naked before the Lord and wrestle in truth—for as long as it takes.

I love to read the words of David and Job in their suffering and grief. The vulnerable honesty before a powerful and mighty God gives me permission to be equally raw and candid in any distress I face.

Read David's lament in Psalm 6:3–7: "*My soul is in deep anguish. How long, LORD, how long? Turn, LORD, and deliver me; save me because of your unfailing love…My eyes grow weak with sorrow.*"

Imagine David crying out to the Lord night upon night, in the depths of his agony, and experiencing only God's silence: "*How long, LORD? Will you forget me forever? How long will you hide your face from me? How long must I wrestle with my thoughts and day after day have sorrow in my heart? How long will my enemy triumph over me?*" (Psalm 13:1–2).

Hear Job's torment through his bitter words:

> "*I cry out to you, God, but you do not answer; I stand up, but you merely look at me. You turn on me ruthlessly; with the might of your hand you attack me. You snatch me up and drive me before the wind; you toss me about in the storm. I know you will bring me down to death, to the place appointed for all the living…Yet when I hoped for good, evil came; when I looked for light, then came darkness…My lyre is tuned to mourning, and my pipe to the sound of wailing.*" (Job 30:20–23, 26, 31)

As you read these words and feel them pry open a tiny chink in your "Christian armour," don't deflect them. Only as you allow yourself to *feel* the longing in your heart to let loose and have it out with God in gut-honesty can you be healed. Don't let the Pharisee in your head judge you and talk you out of wrestling openly with God: *How dare you question God! Who are you to challenge God? God will punish you for your sinful feelings.* Just as Job's friends tried to rebuke him and shut down his laments against God, your own mind and the enemy can plant more guilt to keep you numb. Don't let the echoes of legalism win.

Open up your broken heart to your Father. Could Job have ever resolved his suffering or received God's truth and love if he hadn't lamented as he did? Imagine his anguish; it was far too great to bear without being able to acknowledge his pain before his Father.

The Gift of Emotions

Some of you may have grown up believing that our emotions are the root of much evil, and so our responsibility as mature adults and committed Christians is to keep tight control over them, lest we succumb to temptation. And so the whole idea of "letting it all hang out" with God is completely detestable and foreign to you. It may feel sinful and indulgent, surely not scriptural. It is essential to gently and respectfully correct that thought, because in fact God has designed us to live life fully in love with him with our *hearts,* souls and minds. All emotions are a gift from God. Passion and delight and joy and happiness all come from facing the truth when we're feeling their opposites. Every honest emotion has importance in any relationship, with both God and others. Most of us simply need to learn what they really are and how to express them in a healthy way.

In therapy, we often teach our clients to acknowledge their emotions and accept how they feel *without judgment.* Our emotions aren't "right" or "wrong"; they simply *are.* When we can accept and express them, there is relief, and the negative feelings lose their power to hurt our hearts and destroy others. Unacknowledged emotions always control us in one way or another—the more they are buried and ignored, the greater the power they gain to wreak damage in our lives and the lives of our loved ones.

Our emotions are signals to pay attention to what needs attending to, and we must learn to respond accordingly. They are meant to alert us to what is going on and tell us to do something about it. If you feel angry, that may be your signal to speak up for yourself, to set boundaries or to put a stop to something that is harmful. Ignoring your emotions means forfeiting emotional health and resolution of problems—it means reburying your head in the sand. And unfortunately, as it gets deeper and deeper, more unresolved issues build up and can often escalate into painful crises. Meanwhile, what could have been a molehill can become more like a mountain and ultimately create a lot of havoc for you and everyone around you.

Emotions are incredibly powerful tools, and learning to respect and use them can be at the root of amazing accomplishments. They can release us to be driven by our passions and strong beliefs, but unresolved they are also at the root of consequences as devastating as abuse, self-harm and even murder. It's no wonder that we are taught to stuff them and ruthlessly shut down and ignore how we feel.

Yet recent studies indicate that *all* of our decisions and actions are motivated by our emotions, whether we feel them at a conscious level or not. No matter how logical we may want to be, it turns out that we cannot divorce our decisions from our emotions. And if those emotions are bottled up and pressurized, eventually they'll have to come out. So if we're unaware of our emotions and don't learn to pay attention to our inner world, we can be sabotaged by your emotions time and time again without understanding why and, more importantly, without having enough self-awareness to change the way we respond to a given situation.

Remember, God isn't repulsed by our negative feelings, but because he loves us he wants us to come to *him* to process our emotions and then seek his wisdom to choose how we respond. How we feel is simply how we feel; it isn't "good" or "evil." When we shame our emotions, we end up preventing the processing we need to resolve them. Finding permission to feel what we feel is the key to finally examining and responding well.

Forced to Enter the Wrestling Ring

When I finally let down the walls around my heart and began to be gut-honest with God about feeling betrayed after my brother's death, it was pivotal. I finally began to *experience* God's deep love for me in a way I hadn't ever known.

But as many people find, my life didn't turn around from that day forward. Spiritual renewal is a mountaintop, but when we get back into life, the routine and drudgery make the intimacy fade and grow distant. My lifelong habits of busyness and shoving down my emotions were still there. And truthfully, continuing that deeper heart-investigation work was too frightening and made me feel out of control. Not going there. And so I ran.

I ran for three years. I ran away from facing the emptiness in my soul—the void that was created when I lost my brother and stopped believing in God's love.

Stopped letting myself feel the pain.

But like Jonah, who ran away from God and ended up in the belly of a smelly fish, I was forced to go toe to toe with God. Inexorably, he allowed events to happen in my life that pushed me into the wrestling ring. Like it or not, I was a contender, and regardless of how much I tried to hide in the corner of the ring, God was coming to get me.

The failed business venture and subsequent burnout that took me to the Land of the Unknown were pivotal; they were what finally put me in the ring to wrestle with the Lord. Cornered, with no place to run, I couldn't ignore my pain any longer. Like a cancer that had metathesized throughout my whole life, my pain was engulfing me and preventing me from living the full life God wanted for me.

Why, God?

"Why, God? Why did you lead me to pursue this? Did I hear you wrong? Where did I mess up? Was it all for nought? Did it even make a difference? Have I and everyone I involved paid such a heavy price for absolutely no return?"

Thus began my soul's winter of grief as I began to count the losses. There were so many. As I processed through the pain, I began to realize that my current experience had been triggered by my childhood experiences of abandonment and feeling invisible to others and especially God. I knew that my depression was deeply related to those imprinted feelings because it felt so familiar in its isolation and silence; *I felt like I didn't matter.* My prayers were going nowhere, echoing in the empty space of my soul. It was all too familiar, and before long I remembered: this was exactly how I felt when God took my brother away.

That realization plunged me into the deepest, darkest, coldest place I've ever been—so much despair, I thought I would suffocate. The discouragement felt bottomless and led to such exhaustion, I could hardly get out of bed. Yet even then, I could not give myself any grace.

"There is no pleasure in anything I do," I wrote in my journal during that time.

Everything seems like a chore. All I want to do is escape all demands. I struggle to find any meaning in what I do. I either feel on the edge of tears all the time or I'm numb and lifeless. I am just so tired! I want everyone to leave me alone, stop taking from me, draining the life out of me. I am so sick of faking like I don't feel this way. And then I mock myself for it. My life hasn't been that bad! Who am I kidding? Aside from my brother, no one has died or been seriously ill, I haven't faced any real financial crisis. Nothing that bad has happened. I'm just whining and feeling sorry for myself. But no matter what I do I can't seem to shake myself out of this depression. And I'm so ashamed of being here. I feel like it's all my fault, my personal failure. I'm not spiritual enough to get out. I'm being lazy and irresponsible. I should have known better, but I never do the right thing.

No matter what, I couldn't win for trying.

What stunned me even more—and filled my heart with sorrow—was the slow realization that I had spent much of my life believing I was pursuing what God wanted from me, when I'd really only been trying to gain success to win others' approval. And all of it had only brought me to this point of emptiness. My entire life was futile. In doing what I thought was right, I had completely lost sight of myself. I had mistakenly thought I had to be a "good Christian" and completely lose myself in caring for others. I was left bitter, with a horrible knowledge that it was all for nought. My heart broken, all trust in my Father gone, I realized I had never really known his love for me. I'd wanted to believe I was his daughter and that he had big purposes for my life. But believing I had to remain worthy of it, I'd only slipped further and further away. And unable to ignore the sense of being alone and the fear of that, I had erected for myself instead a religious Tower of Babel life—a self-engineered, self-directed, self-propelled fool's gold of a life I believed was all I could hope for this side of heaven.

Finally, I stopped running. I stopped trying to hide from God the truth of how I really felt about him. I retreated to my trailer, and over a series of weeks, I slept, cried, and journalled. I poured out my heart, page after page. Even so, I was afraid of God's judgment, so I held back. I could tell him of my grief and disappointment, but I couldn't tell him how angry I was, how betrayed I felt by him.

When I finally ventured to ask God what was on his heart for me, he said to me,

"Ah, my child, how you worry! You want so much to be 'perfect' in how you handle things that you forget that I see you. You forget that I know everything about you—nothing takes me by surprise. Be in the moment with me. Allow yourself to be fully naked before me. And accept my perfect love for you. Stop trying so hard to please me! It's in your humanity that you need me. It's in your imperfections that you have been made perfect by my work on the cross."

Well, I decided to take him at his word and so I let it all "hang out," every ugly, dark thought, every shameful feeling. I went on and on, page after page of my journal. And after I'd exhausted myself with it, I waited. And this is what he said to me:

"I'm glad you're here with me, my daughter. I'm glad to be with you. You delight me, regardless of how you're feeling or what mood you're in. I have all the time in the world for you and all the patience in the world. You see, you NEED me. The emptiness in your heart can only be filled by me. No relationship or experience can do that for you. And with me, you can be real—no masks, no pretending. Because my love for you isn't up to you. It JUST IS. I have chosen to place my love on you. Rest in me, and just be. Don't try to talk yourself out of how you feel. Don't try to shut it down. Be aware of it, but don't give in to it. Just give it all to me."

During this season of wrestling, which lasted well over half a year, God peeled me apart layer by layer. He showed me every ugly thought, all the doubts I had, every feeling of betrayal and abandonment that kept me far away from him. As I sat before him, hour after hour, opening my heart before him, he showed me how I'd let my hunger for approval cause me to take on masks so that I'd lost sight of the true me. I had to stop all the posturing, faking and performing.

A New Name

Towards the tail end of this time of wrestling, I read the story of Jacob wrestling with God. For an entire night he fought with God, and he came out with not only a limp but also a new name—Israel. And so I asked the Lord for a new name. "I know my old name was 'People-Pleaser,' 'Mask-Wearer,' 'Approval-Seeker.' So now who am I? What is my new name?"

As I listened quietly, waiting on the Lord, I heard two names in my mind: *Elizabeth* and *Isabel*. Confused, and wondering if this could really be from God, I decided to see what these two names meant. To my shock, I discovered that Isabel is a variant of "Elizabeth," from the Hebrew name "Elisheba," meaning "God's promise." He had purposely given me two names, first, to show me this was from him, since there is no way I could have known they meant the same thing, and second, to demonstrate that he has given me choices in life—Elizabeth or Isabel, but his ultimate will always be the same, and he *will* accomplish what he had purposed in me from the beginning of time, regardless of all I might get wrong.

I then asked the Lord, "What does this mean, Papa? That I am God's promise or you have given me God's promise?"

"Both," he said.

"You are my promise to deliver those I've chosen to be healed, freed and redeemed. You are my representative of my promise to them—out of your ministry to them will be the fulfillment of my promise to them—to bring beauty out of ashes, to redeem that which is so broken and wounded. But I have also promised YOU. From the beginning of time when I marked out your life—I made a promise to you—to claim you as my own, to redeem YOUR life for my purposes. I have made many more promises to you—seek these truths out, hold onto them with absolute surety, find your security in them and in Me, the One who gives these promises. And out of that security, out of resting in me will flow great works, wonderful purposes."

Henri Nouwen, during a time of intense anguish, loneliness and crippling depression, penned these words in his private journal, *The Inner Voice of Love:*

The temptation is to nurse your pain or to escape into fantasies about people who will take it away. But when you can acknowledge your loneliness in a safe, contained place, you make your pain available for God's healing...God wants to touch you in a way that permanently fills your deepest need. It is important that you dare to stay with your pain and allow it to be there...The pain you suffer now is meant to put you in touch with the place where you most need healing, your very heart....Dare to stay with your pain, and trust in God's promise to you.[25]

Make no mistake—it takes fortitude and courage to wrestle with God as Jacob did. You will have to fight against your natural and habitual tendency to flee; I ran for years. There were costs to Jacob's night of struggling with God, and he was left with a permanent disability. He endured great pain. But as Nouwen knew from personal experience, it is only through the time of wrestling that true healing, and coming into your own with your new name—your true calling, your God-given identity—flourishes. And as I've learned, it is only as you move *through* your pain *with* your Father in complete vulnerability and honesty that you come to the next place God has intended for you:

You have to begin to trust that your experience of emptiness is not the final experience, that beyond it is a place where you are being held in love....You have to weep over your lost pains so that they can gradually leave you and you can become free to live fully in the new place.[26]

Digging Deep

Where is your place of pain? Slow down the hectic pace and explore your heart. Check to discover the pains you've been ignoring and allow the Holy Spirit to begin revealing your secret places of loneliness, grief, anger, betrayal and abandonment—all the times you have felt let down by God. Consider the personal history you journalled about in chapter 2, and instead of just writing about it to yourself, write a letter to God. Tell the Lord how you feel as you think about all the pain points of your life. Be honest with how you feel. I promise you, your Father won't judge you!

Ask him to reveal the ways you allowed walls to build around your heart and times when you weren't fully honest with God or yourself. Lay it all out before him by journaling, talking, crying or even shouting out loud. Paint, draw or pound a piano to work it through with your Father—just get real and *talk* to your Father, uncensored and raw. I promise you, God will stay with you through this time of wrestling.

You must finally discover for yourself that God will never let you go.

CHAPTER 13

What's Love Got to Do with It?

Satisfy us each morning with your unfailing love,
so we may sing for joy to the end of our lives.

Psalm 90:14, NLT

Love, love, love. There are more things done in the name of "love" than anything else in the world. We are so besieged by "love" it has become old. The word seems dull.

*I **love** hockey!*

*I **love** chocolate!*

*I **love** Justin Bieber!*

We give it no thought beyond a temporary expression of pleasure. But I have a sneaking suspicion this watered-down, lacklustre version was not God's intent. And maybe we're kind of messed up as a result.

I have something to confess: I enjoy the TV show *The Bachelor.* My husband is completely perplexed by it, but something about that "reality" show just attracts me. I'm a clinical psychologist; I know there are so many things wrong and immoral about the show and I really shouldn't be wasting my time watching it. I keep telling my husband it's research for my counselling of couples, and he just rolls his eyes. But the truth is, I have always been fascinated by how love brings out the best and the worst in us. I analyze the different personalities, try to figure out what makes them tick, and of course I talk to the TV to give them my much-needed advice.

What can I say? It's my calling.

I have to admit another secret: I watch this show because deep within me there's a hopeless romantic rooting for everyone to fall in love and live happily ever after. Given my work as a therapist, I *know* that the statistics on "happily ever after" are not good, and I'm a pawn for the entertainment industry to sell advertising spots. But deep within us, we believe "happily ever after" is more than possible, and many of the choices we make from the time we are young are shaped by that single belief.

No matter how cynical we profess to be about love, and no matter how our ennui anaesthetizes us to it, there is in each of us an inescapable desire to love and be loved. I mean *really* be loved, the kind that never ends. It's how we were created, whether we accept that truth or not. But abandonment, betrayal, hurt, and disappointment make us numb and fight that unquenchable hope of true love. We stuff it down and choose to substitute our anaemic versions—the "love" of stuff, of distractions and pleasures. And all the while we're shutting down our hearts to the possibility of real love.

We sing about it, pray about it and read Scriptures about it, but strangely, our hearts remain unmoved—either because we've "heard that, done that" so many times that it's become meaningless or because we won't let down our guard enough to allow our longings to draw us to the overwhelming passion our Father very much feels.

We know the truth of God's love for us in our heads. But many of us can't seem to receive it in our hearts. Why is that? Of course, there are many reasons. But what is stopping *you* from deeply receiving the love of your Father? In part 1, we reviewed a number of different reasons for disconnects in our relationship with God. I hope you have been able to reflect on what has put that wall up for you. If you haven't, go back to those chapters. Exercise your courage to go deep and do that self-reflection. Until you do, all of this—*all of life*—will remain merely a pleasant theory with little capacity to change your life. They will remain only words, sapped of their power to change—much like *love*.

The Heartbreak of Love

Julian of Norwich expressed it so well:

> Some of us believe that God is almighty and can do everything; and that he is all-wise and may do everything; but that he is all-love and will do everything—there we draw back. As I see it, this ignorance is the greatest of all hindrances to God's lovers."27

Does this resonate with you at all? Truly horrible things do happen in this world, and it's only natural to question God's love. When God doesn't show up again and again, we begin to lose trust in him. He gives and takes away—isn't that what Scripture says? But when God takes away, it *sucks*. It sucks the wind from our sails, the breath from our lungs, the hope from our hearts, the joy right out of living. How can we possibly trust his supposed love for us?

And because we are also in relationship with others, when we experience hurt, heartbreak or betrayals at the hands of people who supposedly care about us, it erodes our capacity to trust in *love* altogether. We are created by God to be in relationship with him and with one another. We are created to receive and give love and to want connection with each other. Our need for relationship is even more powerful than our need for food. In today's time-starved world, we need each other *more,* not less. So why is it that we live in a disconnected society where we have a mere semblance of life together while we rush around in our bubbles, rarely slowing down enough to open our hearts to trust others deeply? Why is it that relationships are as cheap as a trinket on e-Bay and just as disposable? Why do we struggle to persevere in relationships when the going gets tough, when we are hurt and disappointed by others? Why do we automatically assume the worst of each other and, secretly, of God? And why do many of us feel so alone when we are constantly surrounded by people?

Beyond the many philosophical discussions we can have about the human condition, there is a primary biological reason for many of our relationship woes and our inability to love and be loved. Our capacity to develop healthy, secure attachments to God and others is determined by many factors, not least of all our family history. Abandonment, rejection, careless or harsh words, neglect and abuse devastate our ability to experience secure and loving relationships. Having our needs neglected, belittled or stifled really does a number on us. Oh, we may have patched ourselves up and even attained very "successful" lives. But if we're honest with ourselves, we don't believe that God is to be fully trusted.

Just look what God has allowed in our lives. He's the reason we fear so much. *Release control and surrender to him? He must be joking.*

Attachment Is Comfort

We're born knowing absolutely nothing—a blank slate. Our awareness of ourselves grows by our experience of others, and that is shaped by how our caregivers respond to our needs. Our brains are hardwired to learn, neural pathways are ready to be established, and our experiences provide the data. Because we must fully depend on others to care for us, the experiences with our primary caregivers teach us everything we later use in relating to ourselves, each other, and God. Research now shows that our brains' neural pathways are hardwired from our early attachment experiences. God designed relationship with him and others to develop our brains.

Is it any wonder, then, why John said God *is* love?

Research also shows that babies who are consistently touched and spoken to in a loving way are calm; babies who are not are anxious and can become apathetic. We are discovering how dependent a child's developing brain is on its parents, particularly its mother's sensitive, attuned and responsive care. These early experiences literally shape the chemical processes in the brain responsible for how we receive comfort, control our impulses and calm our strong emotions.

From early on, children begin asking critical questions: "Where's Mom? Will she come to me? Can I get to her quickly?" Like a thermostat, this "proximity principle" is a set point for a child's confidence. If he believes Mom is close enough, he is willing to explore the world around him; if he believes Mom isn't close enough, "attachment behaviour" turns on. Attachment behaviour is the attempts to get mother physically closer—for babies, crying or screaming; for kids, whining or acting up to get attention. No child has to learn this behaviour; it's a set program.

Over time, interactions between mother and child become internalized as the attachment style—the *rule* that governs the child's interactions with and beliefs about herself and others. These core beliefs form her beliefs about herself ("Am I worthy of being loved?" and "Am I able to get the love I need?") and her beliefs about others ("Are others trustworthy?" and "Are they available?"). How she responds determine her positive or negative self-image and experience in relationships.

These combined beliefs shape our expectations of future relationships and act as filters, colouring the way we see people and informing them (and us) about how she behaves in relationships. This is called attachment style, and as Milan and Kay Yerkovich describe in their seminal book *How We Love,* how we behave, whether as an avoider, pleaser, vacillator, controller or victim, governs how we attempt to control love.[28]

Regardless of your upbringing, it's important to understand your attachment style and what injuries affected it, because it impacts the way you relate to others and God today. Even those raised in caring homes have experienced various attachment injuries, from something as simple as getting lost to experiencing a time of benign neglect as your parents struggled with other worries or common disappointments when others weren't there for you. This isn't to lay blame but to understand how your early experiences shaped you—so you can grow and change our future. This is part of wrestling with God in the reality of the broken places of your heart.

Relationships That Heal

The good news is, our early attachment styles don't have to sentence us to lifelong relationship difficulties. With God's help, we can overcome the self-defeating patterns of our attachment styles. People raised with a pattern of abuse or abandonment may start to see why they've struggled in relationships for years, which may trigger pain. But if you feel any link between this and what you've been experiencing, I urge you to pursue compassionate Christian counselling. (Speak to your pastor or physician for a referral to a reputable local therapist.) Attachment injury often requires the safety of a therapeutic relationship to resolve and heal.

Deep wounds are *not* something spouses can fully help with, or even close friends. While your loved ones can play a very important role in your healing, attachment injuries create insecurities that can push loved ones away and demand too much from them, which only exacerbates insecurities about rejection. Time with God is essential to healing, yet often the tangible warmth and care of a listening ear with wisdom and encouragement can help us experience God's love. One of my personal mandates as a caregiver is that I represent tangible love to others so they can deeply experience it and begin to internalize it.

In therapy, often for the first time, clients are able to begin changing over time, little by little, through a healthy attachment to their therapist. They begin to heal and develop the emotional capacity (and rewire their neural pathways) to connect well to others. Research bears this out with the science that's rooted in God's complete design. Whether you choose counselling or not, opening your heart and sharing your painful secrets and wounds with others is vital.

Listen to Manning and Hancock:

God calls us every one to come out of hiding. God calls us back from wherever we went running for our lives, calls us back home. God is the *love-crazed* father at the window, waiting for a lost boy to come to his senses, gazing down the road for a sign of his return, now running to meet and embrace and more than half carry his kid the last mile so they can start over, as if nothing bad ever happened between them, as if the party he intends to throw that very night is the celebration of his child's birth.[29] (emphasis mine)

Can you picture that? *Love-crazed?* God is *love-crazed* for *you?*

If those words don't feel real to you, consider whether you have allowed the hurtful experiences in your life to dictate your *loveworthiness.* I know I have. Do you see yourself as a reject or a misfit? Do you see yourself as unlovable? If there's pain in your heart as you read my words, consider whether that pain has attached itself to you through wrong conclusions you have made about yourself. When you feel rejected or unworthy of love, you must be careful not to take on these misbeliefs as part of who you are. God never intends us to suffer because of believing lies. He is a God of truth. Therefore you must see these pains as rooted in lies so that they don't paralyze you or prevent you from loving and being loved. God is love-crazed for *you.* He created you to love and be loved. *You.* And *me.* That is our destiny and our identity, regardless of how life may have tried to convince us otherwise. *Fight* for this truth.

Unprovoked Love

While God does allow pain into our lives—sometimes excruciating and unexplainable pain that we need to wrestle through with him, he *never* desires our pain; nor does he intend for us to experience the pain of believing lies. Our Father is a God of truth, and his heart breaks when we remain trapped, believing lies of our souls' enemy. The truth is that God knows absolutely everything about us— every ugly, broken, sinful, and beautiful, treasured part of us, and he loves us exactly as we are. I love how Mark Buchanan defines God's love in *Hidden in Plain Sight* as "free from conditions." We get so inured to the words "unconditional love" that we forget what that truly means—*free from any and all conditions.* This means that our Father's love for us is completely independent of whether we believe it or not or accept it or not—it just is. As Buchanan writes:

> *Agape* is unprovoked love. It seeks those who never saw it coming, who never *had* it coming, who never sought it out. It shows up unannounced, unexpected, undeserved. It doesn't rise up to our beauty. It doesn't ride in on our popularity. It doesn't depend on our worthiness. It doesn't hang in due to our good manners. It doesn't back off because of our clumsiness, or homeliness, or churlishness. It pursues us, and even when unrequited, pursues us still. It finds us in a ditch and, at personal cost and personal risk, without reward, lifts us up and mends our wounds, and finds us shelter. All unprovoked.[30]

Whether we believe it or not, God loves who we really and truly are. He calls us to come out of hiding just as we are. No amount of spiritual surgery can make us more lovable to God. But instead of believing this to be true, we project onto God our worst beliefs and feelings about ourselves. We fail to believe in God's love because it just doesn't *feel* true. Negative experiences weigh heavily on us and easily override the truth of Scripture and the wonderful spiritual experiences we have. Instead we allow the experiences of the fallen world and the taunts of the enemy to create in us feelings of inadequacy, inferiority and insecurity about our worth. These feelings imprison many of us, keeping us in deep bondage. We know we're sons and daughters of God, but we don't live freely—we don't experience the full life we are intended to have. And so we sleepwalk through our lives.

Digging Deep

So what is going through your mind as you read this chapter? Are you saying, "Yeah, but…"? Fighting to keep up your defences? Longing for this but not believing that it's possible? So what is stopping you from quieting yourself before your Father and asking him to share his heart for *you?* Because you've messed up too badly? Because you believe to the core that there's something wrong with you that makes you somehow unlovable? Could it be that the wounds of your past are causing you to believe lies about yourself?

Ponder what experiences or hurts have built up each brick in the wall around your heart; ask God to show you these bricks. This may be a very painful part for you, so I want you to consider carefully whether you need to do this next part in the safety of a therapeutic relationship. Seek out someone to walk with you through this very important part of your journey. Pray and ask God to lead you to the right person or persons. Do it now; it's time.

Think back to your early years and consider what your home environment was like. What was the emotional climate like in your home? Was it warm and affectionate? Cool and distant? Harsh and angry?

What was your mother like as a mother? How did she show you her love? What was your father like as a father? How did he show you his love? How did your parents show love to one another (if they were together)? How were your emotions handled when you were sad or angry? How did your parents comfort you? How responsive were they to your emotional needs? Were there any other influential adult figures in your life growing up? How did they impact you?

Think about your siblings if you have any. What role did you play in your family? Peacekeeper? Scapegoat? Black sheep? The good child? If you have trouble remembering this, look at some old family photos. Look at the expressions on your faces and the physical contact between you and your family (or lack thereof). Think about how your family of origin is today—the roots of yesterday are often still there today.

If you are experiencing overwhelming pain as you face into the wounding experiences you had as a child, I want you to stop right now. Sit or lie down in a comfortable position. Take a deep breath in through your nose, saying "Maranatha" as you breathe in (it means "Come, Jesus, come" or "The Lord is coming"), hold it for four counts, then breathe out slowly through your nose, saying "Maranatha." Do this for five minutes if you can. You can change the phrases you say in your head, using various four–count sayings: *I love you, Lord. I need you, Lord. Thanks for your love.* Say whatever phrases help you centre on God and calm you.

Then read the following passages (do this even if you're able to complete the family questions; this exercise is great for everyone):

"Do not fear, for I have redeemed you; I have called you by name; you are Mine!…Since you are precious in My sight, since you are honored and I love you…For the mountains may be removed and the hills may shake, But My lovingkindness will not be removed, and My covenant of peace will not be shaken." (Isaiah 43:1, 4; 54:10, NASB)

Speak these words out loud. Carry them with you. Commit them to memory. And as you do, ask God to show you how he feels about you. Even if you don't sense anything at first, be patient like the persistent widow; keep asking him to show you how he feels about you. And then pay attention to what you see, hear, or experience inside of yourself and in the world over the next weeks. Take time to record what you notice and the messages of love he gives you through nature, music, through others around you, and even through the good gifts he gives you. Savour the taste of being loved. Take as long as you need to envelope yourself in the truth of your Father's unprovoked love for you. You were meant to experience it *directly*.

CHAPTER 14

My Father's Beloved

What marvelous love the Father has extended to
us! Just look at it—we're called children of God!
That's who we really are.

1 John 3:1, MSG

I have a secret (I guess not-so-secret now) nickname for my son. I call him "B2"—and when I call him that (which I do frequently), he just smiles in acknowledgement, because he knows it's true. It's what he's grown up hearing and believing about himself. It's become part of his identity, and he doesn't ever question it. *Beloved Boy.* My B2.

The other day, I was hugging my daughter tightly, overwhelmed with love for her. She stayed in my arms for a long time, just soaking it in. Her name is Amanda, meaning "much loved." She too is my beloved child, a gift, who brings me great delight while I watch her mature, celebrate with her when life is good and cry with her when life kicks her down—my baby girl.

I smile with joy when I think about my kids (well, most of the time). What about you? If you've been given the gift of children, does your heart squeeze with love when you think about them? No matter how much they frustrate or test you, do you still see them as your beloved children? *Your* treasured kids.

Can you believe that God sees you the same way? Do you see yourself as your Father's beloved? Can you imagine him smiling in delight over you, rejoicing over you with singing (Zephaniah 3:17)? *We're called children of God! That's who we really are.*

Your birthright. Your identity. *You're the Father's beloved.*

•

Your Story Holds the Handprint of God's Love

In *To Be Told*, Dan Allender tells of the importance of writing down our stories. Beyond what writing our stories teaches us about ourselves, we also gain a clearer image of the handprint of God in the details. Allender asserts that it's only through the telling of our story that we're able to see God's redemption and purposes for our lives—beyond a random assortment of occurrences we've had the good or bad "luck" to experience. Taking the time to look behind us helps us see in front of us, to understand how God has been preparing us for our future and to bring some holy meaning to the most difficult and painful moments of our lives.

In processing through the themes of my story, I was able to see how God was in it at all times, and my perspective of the painful moments in my life shifted. Radically. To my amazement and eternal gratitude, when he gave me my new name, God showed me how he was redeeming my story—not erasing the reality of the pain I had experienced but bringing meaning and beauty out of the ashes of my past.

The themes of my life were loss and emotional abandonment and feeling invisible and forgotten, unvalued, unprotected: *on my own*. Fear entered my life. I saw God as harsh and punitive, and I tried to be good and responsible so that I would avoid his wrath, taking on adult responsibilities too early. I became the helper and the counsellor, always taking care of others at all times, regardless of the personal cost: *I'll be strong for you*. Got to do it for myself, got to get it for myself; no one will do it for me. *It's all up to me*. Approval-seeking, people-pleasing, hiding my true feelings, afraid of disappointing others or letting them down: *I will be who you want me to be*.

And then God entered into my story, and this is what he said:

"You are not alone, I am always with you.
You are not invisible to me.
You are important to me.
I will be strong for you—lean on me.
Don't be afraid—perfect love casts out all fear.
I will take care of you.
I will provide.
I created you—I love and accept who you are, I delight in you.
I want you to be you.
I will restore you—rest in me."

And as the Lord led me to do a deeper study of the meaning of my new name, this is what I discovered to my incredulous delight: some additional meanings of the name "Elizabeth" beyond "God's promise":

- *I am God's daughter (precious, valued, known).* Therefore, I am *not* on my own, nor do I have to be whoever others want me to be. I already have an identity that can never be stolen. I can be the me God created me to be.
- *God is my sustenance (strength).* I don't have to be strong for others. I don't have to lose myself trying to take care of others. I *can* rest in him no matter the circumstances, and he *will* sustain me.
- *God is my abundance (generous provider).* It's *not* all up to me. God is there for me and he will take care of me and generously provide, I don't have to do it all myself.

By giving me my new name of *Elizabeth,* God shone the light of truth on the lies I believed through the painful themes in my life. He already knew my story, and he knew the sorrow and loss I would experience. Even while he wept with me, he was already preparing for me a tender and perfect response to my painful story. He *has* redeemed my story and is bringing purpose to the dark and painful aspects of my life, and I see the sheer beauty and hope and love that has been woven into every single teeny-tiny piece of this life of mine.

What about your story? Can you see God's handprint woven throughout it? Can you see how you were chosen as his beloved before the beginning of time? Every aspect of your story—past, present and future—speaks of God's love for you and your identity as his child.

You Are the Beloved

I don't know about you, but I have a hard time wrapping my head and heart around the truth that this great, big, holy, unknowable, all-powerful, awe-inspiring, incomprehensible God of ours loves *me* and is intimately involved in the tiny details of my life. It's hard for us to grasp that degree of perfect love and the value we have in God's eyes, particularly when faced with the intimate knowledge we have of our hidden flaws and sinful thoughts and compulsions and when battered about by the scorn and rejection of the world. It's almost impossible for us to anchor ourselves in the truth of our identity as our Father's beloved, especially given the competing din and lies we hear in the messy, painful and broken pieces of our lives. Listen to the words of John Eagan as he quotes the words of his spiritual director and is transformed by the power of this truth: "*Define your-self radically as one beloved by God.* God's love for you and his choice of you con-stitutes your worth. Accept that, and let it become the most important thing in your life"[31] (emphasis mine).

Can you hear your Father's voice calling out this truth to you?

Henri Nouwen, a man deeply acquainted with sorrows, who struggled with deep depression, loneliness and feelings of rejection, after wrestling with the whys and hows of his life came to this simple yet profound conclusion:

> I have come to realize that the greatest trap in our life is not success, pop-ularity, or power, but self-rejection. Success, popularity, and power can indeed present a great temptation, but their seductive quality often comes from the way they are part of the much larger temptation to self-rejection. When we have come to believe in the voices that call us worth-less and unlovable, then success, popularity, and power are easily per-ceived as attractive solutions. The real trap, however, is self-rejec-tion...Self-rejection is the greatest enemy of the spiritual life because it contradicts the sacred voice that calls us "Beloved." Being the Beloved constitutes the core truth of our existence.[32]

He goes on to say,

> All I want to say to you is, "You are the Beloved," and all I hope is that you can hear these words as spoken to you with all the tenderness and force that love can hold. My only desire is to make these words rever-berate in every corner of your being—"You are the Beloved."[33]

Can you hear the words of your Father, "You are my beloved"? Stop right now in the middle of the busyness of your life; put aside all of your neuroses, self-doubts, self-rejection and anxieties. Pause long enough to listen to the words of your Father: "You are my beloved."

This is what we all deeply long for. We yearn to know we are adored, that we are special and loved *uniquely,* not in a generic way. We want to know *we matter.* That we hold a special place in our Father's heart, a place no one and nothing can ever rival or take away from us. Jesus loves *me,* this I *know.* Without this certainty in the core of our being, we will misinterpret every painful aspect of our story, just like I did before God redeemed my story and gave me a fresh perspective. But I could only receive that new truth after I accepted his love and my identity as his beloved.

Otherwise, the sorrow that God allows in our lives will feel like abandonment or cold-heartedness on his part. Without this foundation of knowing we're our Father's beloved, we will move precariously through life, trying to prove our worth and earn belovedness through approval, performance or achievement.

I can't stress the importance of this truth enough: don't rush through this. Pause and listen to what your Father wants to say to you, right now. If you don't stop to receive this truth, *all* of your life will be lived out of this place of deficit, of insecurity. All of your experiences, all of your relationships—everything in your life—will be coloured by your negative expectation that God is out to get you, no one could ever love you, and everything and everyone will let you down. All of the pain in your life will be because God is your betrayer, not your lover. He has sucker punched you.

I can't even begin to explain why God allows the pain in our lives, why human suffering is on such an unbelievable, horrific grand scale. But I can tell you that the only antidote, the only power to transform, the only possible way to redeem our pain, is God's irreplaceable, perfect, unchanging, immense, irreversible love for us. Love is God. God is love. Stand certain in your identity as his Beloved—much loved, desired, wanted, chosen, treasured.

You must get this picture of what this truth means. Consider the words of Manning and Hancock:

> This is the Big Idea: *Define yourself radically as one totally loved by God.* Right now. As-Is. Not to be left like this, certainly, but just as certainly never to be loved, valued, cherished any more or less than you are in this very moment because God's love doesn't depend on you. So please, please, please stop running away when you mess up and run into the arms of the one who totally loves you as you are right now.[34]

The One Jesus Loved Dearly

The other day, while reading the familiar passage in John 13 when Jesus was spending time with his disciples just before he went to the cross, it struck me anew how our identity as his beloved is key to how God sees us.

After washing his disciples' feet, Jesus was reclining around the table with one of his closest friends, John. In verse 23, John writes of himself, *"One of his disciples, **the one Jesus loved dearly**, was reclining against him, his head on his shoulder"* (MSG, emphasis mine). In fact, throughout his Gospel, John repeatedly referred to himself as the one Jesus loved. In John 19:26, *"Jesus saw his mother and **the disciple he loved**"* (MSG); in 20:2, John describes himself as *"the other disciple,* *the one Jesus loved*"; further in 21:7, "*Then **the disciple Jesus loved** said to Peter*" (MSG); and in 21:20, "*Peter noticed **the disciple Jesus loved** following right behind*" (MSG, emphasis mine).

I especially love the description of John in the Amplified version of John 13:23 as one whom Jesus loved, whom he esteemed and delighted in. These are precious words of Jesus' deep love for his friend. John was a simple and uneducated man of humble beginnings and no great import. What a powerful way to describe oneself! He walked daily with Jesus and opened himself up to him to the point where he reclined with his head on Jesus' shoulders or bosom. John's intimate relationship with Jesus defined him as the one Jesus loved dearly.

Thomas Merton says it succinctly: "If I make anything out of the fact that I am Thomas Merton, I am dead…Quit keeping score altogether and surrender yourself with all your sinfulness to God who sees neither the score nor the scorekeeper but only *his child* redeemed by Christ"[35] (emphasis mine). His child. My Father's beloved. Period.

Nothing is more important than capturing well the core of your belovedness.

Digging Deep

Your Father's love for you and his purposes are woven into every aspect of your story. Review what you wrote down in chapter 2, and consider how you've described your family in chapter 13. What are the themes of the broken parts for you? Abandonment? Rejection? Loneliness? Shame?

Now take the time to think about all the good experiences of your life—the blessings, the unexpected opportunities, all of the high points. To help you organize this, you may find it helpful to draw a timeline. At the far left of the line write "birth," and at the far right of the line put your current age. Then as you consider all of the experiences of your life, both good and bad, you can plot them on your lifeline. All of the positive experiences are plotted on top of the line and all of the negative ones are written below the line—like mountaintops and valleys.

Will you take the time to enumerate the experiences of your life, both good and bad, so that you can see God's handprint all through it? If you struggle to do this on your own, consider doing it with a mentor, a counsellor or a wise friend you can ask to meet with.

As painful as remembering the challenges and trials you've endured may be, remember that for every loss, injury or hurt, he has an answer. God has given a promise for your future that transforms the sorrow and pain of your past. He grieves with you and will show you the truth of his care embedded in your past.

And knowing how God has been there throughout your story allows you to trust that he will be there in your future. But to know that, you have to look. So will you?

Go back now over your lifeline and *see* the handprint of God. Prayerfully ask your Father to show you. What are *his* answers to the themes of your life? You can write it down, or if you're more creative, use pictures, stickers and song lyrics. Put them throughout your lifeline to help you see the hand of God throughout your life.

Will you choose to seek out the truth of his great love for you? Will you choose to accept your identity as our Father's beloved? If not, what is preventing you from doing so? Ask the Lord to reveal your heart to you and show you the barriers to accepting your true identity as his beloved.

CHAPTER 15

The Whole Truth and Nothing but the Truth

Jesus said, "If you hold to my teaching, you are really my disciples. Then you will know the truth, and the truth will set you free."

John 8:31–32

Larry shook his head wearily as he looked bleakly out the window. He could no longer make eye contact with me, because he was feeling so defeated. "I've tried everything," he said. "Every twelve–step program, tons of men's Bible studies, men's events…I've got books upon books sitting on my shelf. Nothing works! Why am I feeling so stuck?" As I listened to Larry, I felt empathy for him. I knew that Larry had come to a critical point in his journey, where "the rubber meets the road," and I knew that the next steps he took would be crucial ones.

You see, Larry was what I call a "knowledge junkie." He was well educated, read many books, attended many seminars, knew a lot about the human condition and could quote aptly from the Bible. He stayed on top of the latest research and news, and he had attended so many Bible studies that he could teach the classes himself. But most of what he learned remained just that, head knowledge. Every time he tried to take steps forward, he would listen instead to his feelings and would give in to feelings of defeat. As with all people who struggle to change, Larry was driven primarily by his feelings and not by the *truth* of what he was learning through all of his studies. It wasn't until he was able to identify the lies he believed, replace them with the truth, and begin to *live* out of that truth—take *action* based on truth—that he was finally able to move forward and change the trajectory of his negative feelings, which had long held him back. It was when he began to replace believing the father of lies with believing the Father of truth that he began to walk in freedom.

John Eldredge captures this human tendency well in his book *Walking with God:*

Everlasting love—that cuts right through the lie that love never stays. His love does. It is everlasting. Immoveable. True. We don't believe the Scriptures because they don't seem to align with what we are *feeling* right now…We are so stubborn in our unbelief because we aren't at that moment *experiencing* whatever it is God says is true. He knows that we make agreements with all sorts of lies, distortions, and accusations. Now he invites us to agree with him on what is *true.*[36]

Our Own Source of Truth

In today's society, truth is defined by what feels good to us, what we choose to believe. The individual has become the ultimate source of truth, and our individual reasoning has become the god of truth-seeking. Our pride can deceive us into thinking we are the source of our own truth. I remember hearing fiction writer and speaker Frank Peretti on the radio years ago, talking about the foolishness of relativism, using the analogy of being in a dark room.

Picture yourself in a huge dark room. It's a featureless room with nothing to guide you or tell you where you are or where you are going. You're walking around in the dark, trying desperately not to bump into anything or anyone. But then, suddenly, you feel something…it's a chair! It has a back and legs, and you can easily sit on it. Now, you can use this as a sort of home base to reach out and discover where you are in the room. It is a *fixed point of reference.* As long as it doesn't move, you can navigate without getting lost. But as soon as you pick it up and make it a part of your mobility and consciousness, it isn't a fixed point of reference anymore.

Absolute truth is like that chair. It doesn't change, it is separate from us, and it is the basis on which we order our lives. For the Christian, that fixed point of reference is God revealed through the Bible. It is the standard by which we judge people's actions, especially our own. For relativists and many North Americans today, that chair could be their mind, reason, or some intuitive sense inside them. The relativist's chair has wheels on it. It can change whenever society decides it's time for some new ethics.

Even as Christians, we can easily fall prey to believing our own perceptions and making decisions out of those feelings, rather than on the truth of God's Word. And one of the truths that we seem to struggle with—and that we desperately need to anchor us—is the truth of God's perfect love for us and our identity as his beloved children.

The Blurry View Through Our Filters

Research shows that we all filter how we see ourselves, others, the world and even God through life experiences. The conclusions we draw shape our filters. If my filter is negative and I believe people will hurt and reject me, then my experience of life is negative. This is in fact what happened to Larry.

Many people have *faulty filters* that tell them false things about themselves and life, based on how other people have treated them. If I got criticized a lot as a child, the conclusion is that I can never measure up. Often these false beliefs are so subtle that people don't even realize they're there. *Here's how you can tell you have a faulty filter: if you continually feel crummy about yourself or feel strong reactions to a situation where that emotion is illogical.*

Many of us will experience hurtful encounters throughout our lifetime. As children we didn't have the capacity to draw the correct interpretations on our own: *Oh, that's just Mommy having a bad day.* Or, *Joey is just being mean; it's not true when he calls me stupid.* Deeply egocentric, kids always see themselves as the centre of their universe; therefore it must be their fault if something bad happens to them. They also automatically believe whatever adults tell them, so if their parents blame them or call them names, that becomes truth to them. That's why kids *need* loving adults to help them navigate through life and understand reality. Without this loving guidance, they will develop faulty filters. Wrongly interpreted, life presents lies to people about themselves and causes an unbelievable amount of pain. This is one of the leading causes of emotional and psychological problems today.

For example, I have a client who was sexually abused by her father from the time she was a very little girl until she was an adolescent. The pains she bears are from the lies she's believed about herself. I can reason with her and tell her how beautiful and precious she is, and she may even agree with me intellectually. But because she believes the lie that she is dirty and worthless, every time her husband is less than kind to her she's devastated, believing that he can't love her, because she's dirty and worthless.

God does allow pain in our lives for many reasons. But he *never* wants us to experience pain as a result of believing lies. He is the God of truth. It is his will for us to live in truth and to be free as a result. Jesus said in John 8:32, "*Then you will know the truth, and the truth will set you free.*" But the verse before is one we often forget yet is so key to our freedom: "*If you **hold** to my teaching*" (John 8:31). The word "hold" is an active verb, which requires some action on our part. We have to consistently hold onto the truth of what Scripture tells us. I especially like the Amplified version of verse 31: "*If you abide in My word [hold fast to My teachings and live in accordance with them], you are truly My disciples*" (AMP). It is *living* in the truth that sets us free, not the mere *knowledge* of the truth.

For As You Think, So You Are

Many of us are in bondage to lies we believe about ourselves, about others, about life, about God. And because our thoughts act as a filter through which we view our world and our circumstances, believing lies is deadly. Our *thoughts* about a given situation, *not* the situation itself, determine our emotional reactions. Proverbs 23:7 says, "*For as [a man] thinks within himself, so he is*" (NASB). Imagine a friend seeming to ignore you. If you believe she simply didn't see you, you would likely dismiss the incident. But if you believe she deliberately ignored you, it will trigger anger or sadness and probably both.

Many relationships are destroyed on as simple a basis as that. Sadly, many people, including me, struggle with negative filters about God, which prevent us from experiencing his love and the peace and joy that comes from knowing and living out of the truth about God and his tender love for us.

A few years ago I was aching with shame and sadness over my sinful heart. I was beating myself up badly for my inability to break free from the sin in my life. I had just heard a pastor preaching on godly sorrow versus worldly sorrow ("*Godly sorrow brings repentance that leads to salvation and leaves no regret, but worldly sorrow brings death*" [2 Corinthians 7:10]), and he said that if we really focused on how we grieved God's heart when we sinned, it would move us to let go of our sinful patterns. So I began to chastise myself: if I really had godly sorrow about my sin and hated breaking God's heart, wouldn't I stop?

As I was sinking deeper into the morass of my self-flagellation, a part of me recognized that I was falling prey to wrong thinking, that there were some lies or mental agreements that were affecting my emotions and my actions. And so I began to pray that God would reveal these lies to me, and this is what I heard:

I can never break free from my sin.
I'm doomed.
I'm hopeless to change.
It's all up to me and I can't do it.
I'm a fraud and a fake.
I'm bad.
I will forever keep messing up.

And then when I asked the Lord for the truths that he wanted to share with me to replace these lies, he shared these thoughts with me:

The truth will set me free—sin no longer has its hold on me.
I am redeemed.
God will change me—he *will* complete the good work he has begun in me.
It's not up to me; God will help me.
I'm a beloved daughter of the Most High King.
I am holy and blameless in God's eyes.
I can do all things through Christ who gives me strength.

I began to speak these words of truth out loud, repeating them as many times as necessary, for two reasons: firstly, I have found that accessing information in two ways—both mentally and aurally—helps my brain to solidify the truth; and secondly, I am fighting a spiritual battle and have found that truths spoken out loud have greater power to defeat the lies of the enemy. As Jesus did in the desert when he was being tempted by Satan, speaking Scripture out loud gives the enemy no choice but to depart. After this, my emotions calmed right down, and a sense of peace came over me. I have found that this practice helps me consistently centre myself back in God and his truths, so that my negative emotions no longer have a hold on me. Taking the time to do this whenever my negative emotions are triggered has helped me avoid their effects.

The Power of Your Thoughts

Ample research shows that depressed people regularly see the world in negative ways. People who struggle with fear and anxiety see the world as frightening and overwhelming. Negative self-talk is pervasive in emotional distress, depression and anxiety. The key to better understanding our emotions is to realize that they aren't based on what is happening to us but what we *think* is happening to us. For example, if we thought an intruder was trying to open the door, how would our emotional responses differ from if we thought it was merely our son? The emotions are real enough; we'd feel genuine fear or despair, not because of the situation but because of the way we'd interpreted it.

We can't control many of our circumstances, and trying to focus and control our external situations can leave us exhausted and defeated. We *can* control what we *tell* ourselves about our circumstances. We can also choose to focus on the *external* source of all truth, God, rather than our feelings and thoughts.

Truth isn't something we learn; truth is *Someone* we know. Jesus says that he is the truth (John 14:6). Truth changes people's hearts and lives. The Scriptures are our only reliable source of truth.

God Is the Truth

One of the greatest joys for me as a therapist is watching how God works in a heart to change and heal someone. I love to work with people who come with tender, teachable hearts, who are longing to draw close to God and learn the truth. The transformations I've had the privilege to witness are incredible and such a joy to watch. With God's guidance, I usually start by helping the person to identify the lies he or she believed, then move on to repent of sinful actions and attitudes that have resulted from believing these lies, then learn the truths to replace those lies, and finally learn how to live those truths in his or her life on a daily basis.

Because God is truth, a necessary part of our journey of healing is drawing close to him and growing in our intimacy with him. But in the end, we have to choose: We have to believe in God, who is truth, rather than our emotions, or the lies of the enemy. There are two key principles in John 8:31–32: (1) take action—"*If you keep on obeying what I have said*" (CEV) and (2) focus on the truth—living life out of the truth that God has revealed to us. Here again is this very important truth: we need to take *action*. We need to develop some "head" knowledge through reading, listening, observing godly mentors, or counselling. And as we learn, we need to begin applying the head knowledge to our lives by taking baby steps every day.

As a therapist, I can do nothing to change your life. You must choose to apply what you're learning and apply your insight consistently. Only you have the power to make that change. Not even God will do that for you, because he's more concerned about your maturity than your dysfunction and pain.

And you must *persevere*. Imagine when you were a toddler and just learning to walk—what if the very first time you fell down, you concluded that this walking thing didn't work, so you just sat down? Can you imagine? You would never be able to walk or run or dance. You would be trapped and unable to know the freedom of being mobile.

Continue applying what you've learned *no matter how you feel*. Anger will try to prevent you from forgiving someone and restoring a relationship; hurt will encourage you to avoid or hurt back the person; fear will hold you back from confronting the issue or setting healthy boundaries. But each baby step forward changes the trajectory of your life and your relationship with God.

God has given us a very precious love letter in the Bible. The Bible also tells us about God's character and all the promises he's given us as his children. But all too often, instead of understanding God's character as who he is, we interpret him through our circumstances. I have a client who has yet to make the step of faith for Christ, because she still struggles with accepting that a good God would allow her father to abuse her so terribly. She cried out to God many times to make him stop. Her life is one of fear and bitterness and loneliness because she is using her circumstances to define who God is.

God is calling out to you to get to know him personally. Begin by asking him to reveal himself to you, and get to know his character. Read the Bible regularly, with the intent of mining out the traits of God and his promises to you. There are many Bible studies that can help. Neil Anderson has a very helpful list of the characteristics of God in his book *The Bondage Breaker*.[37] Break each of these down and meditate on the quoted Scriptures, one per day, and then when you're done, do it again, and again, until these truths are ingrained upon your mind.

Digging Deep

Now we come to a critical point in your journey. Hopefully, if you've been engaging in the process of working through your own history and the ways you disconnect from God, you are now ready to face down the lies and wrong mental agreements that have blocked you from believing the truth of God's Word and his love for you. As you do the following exercise, make sure that you give yourself enough time to fully engage—don't rush through this in between other appointments. And if you find it difficult to process on your own or need accountability to stay focused, consider inviting a trustworthy friend, pastor or counsellor to help you with this.

Ready?

Grab your journal and a pen (or use your computer), and begin to still yourself before God. Begin by praying,

Lord, I come before you now, confessing that I have believed lies about myself, about you and about others. Please forgive me, Father. I long to know the truth. Please protect my time with you from the attempts of the enemy to thwart this and keep me in bondage to his lies. Send as many angels as are needed to protect me, and even now, sweep through this entire room and remove any evil that may be trying to cause disruption or harm to me. I want only your truths, Lord.

Holy Spirit, I invite you now to come and guide me in this process. Help me feel what you want me to feel, see what you want me to see, hear what you want me to hear. Come now, Lord Jesus. I place this time in your hands.

Now with your journal and pen in hand, pray, "Lord, please reveal to me now, any lies or wrong mental agreements that I have held." Then write down whatever comes to your mind. Continue on until you have a sense that you have come to the end—at least at this point (you may find that God will lead you to do this exercise multiple times as you continue on in your journey when he feels you are ready to deal with certain strongholds in your life).

Once you have completed the list of wrong mental agreements, say the following out loud:

In the name of Jesus Christ of Nazareth, I renounce the beliefs, thoughts and attitudes I have held in my mind when I committed to agree with myself that _____ [list all of the mental agreements that the Lord brought to mind earlier]. I break the power, authority, effects and consequences of these agreements in my life and I declare them to be null and void. They are all broken now in the name of the true Lord Jesus Christ of Nazareth. I also renounce any curses or vows I may have made with myself, either knowingly or unknowingly. Lord, please show me what truths you have for me to replace these wrong mental agreements.

Again, write down everything that God brings to mind, asking him for more until you sense that there is no more. Once you have your new list, pray,

I replace all of my wrong mental agreements with the truth that _____ [list all the truths that God has brought to your mind]. I choose to live out of the truths that you have revealed to me. Thank you, Father, that you are the God of truth and that you have given me the Holy Spirit to lead me to all truth. Help me to continue living in your truth and to be free.

Remember, it is a *daily* choice to walk in God's truth, and often it won't be easy. Left unchecked, we will naturally veer towards our old way of thinking. We must continuously track our sense of well-being to determine when we are being negatively drawn towards believing the old lies again. And as I said earlier, the Lord may lead you to do this process once again as he peels back the layers and continues to change you into the person he's created you to be—beloved, chosen and free.

CHAPTER 16

Enough Is Enough

"Steep your life in God-reality, God-initiative, God-provisions. Don't worry about missing out. You'll find all your everyday human concerns will be met."

Matthew 6:33, MSG

I was completely fed up. I paced back and forth in my trailer, making my list of "to-dos"—everything I had to pack up, clean up, ship out. The sunshine beckoning me to the beach only increased my peevish mood. No time for idle rest.

I was literally days from returning to work from my three-month sabbatical, and let me tell you, I wasn't ready. I had no answer, no clarity, no new direction, no "aha" from God. *Where is this light to guide my path, Lord? Am I just supposed to go back to the same old? You know what trouble that got me into.*

I was sick of being in the Land of the Unknown—the land where my old compasses of performance, achievement and approval no longer worked. Everything I used to rely on was slowly being peeled away.

Do you ever feel that way? Like God has stripped everything away from you, and then when he finally has your attention and you're ready for some answers, he leaves you hanging? And for someone like me—goal-oriented, driven, always-have-to-have-a-plan—it was excruciating. *Answers, God, I need answers! You hear me?*

I realized later that God was showing me the many idols in my heart. It was a scary place: I had no control, and I felt forgotten by him. He seemed not to care to answer my prayers. He'd left me hanging with nothing left. Yet all the time, he was teaching me that he is enough. Just God, the Provider—not his provision. Just God, the Almighty—not what he does for me. Just God, my Father—not all the privileges he gives me as his daughter. It was only when the old things had finally died away and I stopped fighting long enough to listen that he asked, "Am I enough for you, my child?"

The next day, I woke up in a foul mood after a sleepless night, fretting about returning to work. *What am I going to do?* My journaling that morning took on a dark tone:

> Are you there, God? Do you even hear my prayers? In this Land of the Unknown when you are silent in response to my prayers and pleas for answers, I am left hanging in the wind, susceptible to every storm that comes my way, up and down with my emotions and fears. Being in this land is stirring up feelings of being forgotten, of not being important. Again, I am left alone to deal with things on my own. Where are you when I need you?

As I allowed myself to feel the depth of my painful emotions, the vent finally burst forth:

> I am SO tired of being patient and waiting in the ambiguity of the Unknown!! I'm so tired of the pressure of balancing everyone's demands and needs and not knowing what you want me to do! What do you want from me??
>
> I feel so out of control, like I don't have a voice—that what I think or want doesn't matter. I think I'm so fearful of being outside your will that I'm afraid to speak up. I'm so afraid of being a whining, complaining follower that I try to stay quiet and ignore my feelings, just pretending I'm okay. Well, I'm not okay! And I'm tired of feeling ignored! I'm tired of suppressing my feelings and not being honest with how I feel. IT STINKS BEING IN THE LAND OF THE UNKNOWN!! I'm angry. I'm hurt and I'm so discouraged. I hate feeling this way. And I hate feeling like a bad Christian for feeling this way. I want to say, "Enough already!" Help me, Papa! I feel like I'm drowning in all the confusing thoughts and feelings. Papa, please, what would you say to me? Please speak to me.

I waited in silence for a time, breathing in short bursts, heart beating rapidly. My hands shook from the intensity of my emotions. I sat stiffly in my pajamas on the edge of the bed in my trailer, gripping my pen fiercely. Tears were pouring down my face, and I knew I looked a fright—hair lank and hanging around my face, fraying pajamas that were grey from too many washes, ripe morning breath.

Great way to meet with the Almighty. I glared at my sole companion, a buzzing fly that was distracting me from my burning bush moment.

After a beat, God spoke: "Be still and know that I am God. Where were you when I formed the earth? When I fashioned the sky and the seas? Do you not know that I am the LORD your God? Peace."

Learning to Listen

What? I wanted to scream.

That's it?! No answers to my questions?

But even as I fought a rising discouragement, peace grew in me, quickening my spirit. We were finally getting to the crux of what the Lord was teaching me. And I found a resolve—not from having any answers but because I knew that God was *there* and would always be with me. Somehow the Lord would always work out the messiness of my broken life. I knew God was teaching me to let go and trust, that he hadn't forgotten me or dismissed my concerns as unimportant. I knew, too, that my Father was in the process of healing me from my wounds of abandonment as he taught me about his perfect love, even if I couldn't see or understand it.

And in that space of peace and acceptance, I finally let go, and God said,

"I am a jealous God, and I want *all* of you. I want all of your heart. I want to heal your heart and I've always known you struggle to fully trust my love. I understand why—but it is not good for you. You do not stand alone for I am ALWAYS with you. I will never abandon you, my beloved one. This is a lie of the enemy. I know your desires and longings and I will meet them if you delight yourself in me. This has never been about an answer to your questions or problems; it has always been about our relationship. About teaching you to surrender fully to my love for you— you are so precious to me. About how I long for you to know the depths of my love and know what I can do in and through your life when you let go and stop grasping for control. Love is patient and has let you "have your way" but now the time has come for you to see that my way is best—your way has only kept you from all that could be. Now it is time for that to change. Trust me, my child, and rest. In my love, you will see how light my yoke is. Revel in me and in our relationship and you *will* experience deep joy and peace regardless of the circumstances. I *am* enough for you."

Do you hear that? God *is* enough for you. But because he is love, God will not force you to accept that. Annie Dillard says it succinctly in *Teaching a Stone to Talk:* "God does not demand that we give up our personal dignity, that we throw in our lot with random people, that we lose ourselves and turn from all that is not him…It is a life with God which demands these things."[38] A life with God is a life finding out that God is sufficient, where we lose ourselves and turn from everything that isn't him. It's *all* about God. Rather than being the restrictive or harsh thing we've imagined, a life with only God is a life of freedom and peace, because it is the life we were created to live. I know that in my head, but boy, is it hard to live out in reality! Yet time and time again, when I choose to surrender to God, I have always reaped the benefits of that decision. Looking back at my time in the Land of the Unknown, it was one of the best times of my life—I bear humble testimony to the peace and joy that result in finally surrendering to my Father and accepting that *he is enough.*

Hard to Let Go

It's hard to let go, isn't it? Truly, it would be foolish to let go if you didn't have absolute assurance of God's love for you, his goodness and his sovereignty over your life. It would be like surrendering to some deity up there who seems harsh, fickle or uncaring. Unless you have a personal experience with God of his reclaiming love—either directly or through someone who has shown you his love through their care—then I'd say don't do it. But don't cheat yourself of a life-changing encounter with your Father. He is waiting with open arms to *pour* his love over you, to fill your emptiness with his fullness. He is waiting to reclaim you as his Beloved.

If you don't yet have this assurance of God's love for you, I *urge* you, go back to chapters 13 and 14. Reread those chapters; go as slow as you need to—mine those chapters for truths about God's love for you. Don't read these chapters superficially, just for information—choose to *experience* them. Do the deep-rooted heart stuff, and I promise you, the answer you've been looking for will be there.

I know how hard this can be. I think back to my Christian journey: when I first met Christ, I accepted him as my Saviour because, frankly, I just wanted to stay out of hell. Then I started to believe that Jesus just might be the thing to make my life happy, safe and carefree. He could be like my personal genie to grant all my desires and wishes. After all, I reasoned, Jesus wants me to be happy right? So my focus was on all the things I wanted: a happy marriage, a successful career, beautiful and perfect children, good health, prosperity.

So you may be able to imagine my anger and distress when life didn't turn out the way I believed it would with God at the helm. Imagine my fear when I realized that bad things do happen to Christians—*really* bad things. What was going on? Was it worth it? Following Christ is hard, and if it does not really produce the dividends, why should we even want it? Why does God let so many difficult things happen to the children he professes to love?

Nothing about this is easy.

When life doesn't go our way, at times we can't help but to ask why. One of the most difficult lessons I had to learn is that God doesn't ask us to understand him—he asks us to *trust* him and his perfect love for us. This is a point around which many believers get stuck. When they experience great pain in life, they want God to tell them why, and they get very angry at God. But even knowing the answers won't comfort us. This is hard. In times of suffering, answers won't ease the pain. Only the Lord himself can do it. And if our trials turn us to him, that's all the answer we really need. All we need is him.

The hardest burden I bear as a therapist is seeing the devastating pain of my sisters and brothers, and there's nothing I can say or do to take that pain away. During those times, I know all I can do is cry with them. What keeps me on with the work I do is my hope that God will reveal himself with and in and through his people who comfort. I pray to believe it is his good and perfect will to give them *this* answer and *not* the answers they are seeking to their suffering.

I remember early in my career counselling a father who had just lost his son to suicide. All the "what ifs" he asked himself, all the "whys" he asked God—it was one of the most painful times I've ever experienced as a therapist, and as I listened to him keening for his son, his pain made even more unbearable as he ruminated on all the ways he could have stopped it, the ways *God* could have prevented it, I felt so overwhelmed, so helpless in the face of his devastation. That experience marked me. How do you comfort someone with answers you don't have? How do you point to God when you yourself can't comprehend how he allows such suffering? How can we—as Christ followers—ever truly reconcile the love of God with what he allows in this world?

And then, even as I think it, I'm reminded: God himself willingly allowed his Son to "commit suicide." He allowed Jesus to knowingly walk to his brutal death. He who had the power to stop his murder chose instead to endure the incomprehensible pain of losing his son—out of love for *us*, his other children. How he must have suffered at the loss, and how deeply he must understand our worst suffering and most helpless sorrow. Do you know that when Jesus was dying on the cross, *your* face was in his mind's eye, *your* name was on his lips? Do you really know that your Father chose to suffer for *you?* Will you allow the truth of such a great love comfort you during your time of sorrow, in your Land of the Unknown?

Will Christ Be Enough?

Here's a really tough question I want you to ask yourself: Do you love God for *who* he is or for *what* he can do for you? If you lost everything, would Christ be enough for you even over the pain of all you lost? We all profess to love him, yet how many of us can say it this truthfully? How about when God is silent and doesn't give us the answers or the relief from our problems that we want; do we still trust him then? Troubles will come and test our relationship with God sooner or later, and our faith in him will be on trial.

So this is critical for us to remember: We can't define God by what happens in our lives. If something good happens, that's no more evidence of his loving-kindness than if something bad happens. Our labels on what happens are a reflection of our *feelings,* not the truth of God's character or his promises to us. If we concluded that God is too weak to combat the evil of this world or doesn't love us enough, we'd be lost.

We can't control everything that happens or even understand why it happens. When we insist on knowing why, we cut off our growth and lose our way in the journey to knowing God and his heart for us. Beyond "why?" we need to ask, "What is God doing *in* me through the troubles he's allowing in my life?" Don't get me wrong: ask why, and keen in your pain and anger with God—he will not break. You need to experience this essential step in getting real and authentically connecting with your Father. But if we hold out on him because we're waiting for an answer to our why, we are the ones who miss out on the healing and growth he wants for us.

We have to remember that God's perspective is different from ours. We tend to judge the rightness of a decision by the outcome (positive outcome = right; negative outcome = wrong). We are more concerned with our temporal happiness, while God is more concerned with his eternal purposes; he uses both our "good" and "bad" choices to lead us to greater maturity. God's ultimate will is to bring us into intimate relationship with him and conform to the image of Christ, rather than ensuring our happy and trouble-free life.

Immediately Jesus made His disciples get into the boat and go ahead of Him to the other side to Bethsaida, while He Himself was sending the crowd away. After bidding them farewell, He left for the mountain to pray. When it was evening, the boat was in the middle of the sea, and He was alone on the land. Seeing them straining at the oars, for the wind was against them, at about the fourth watch of the night He came to them, walking on the sea; and He intended to pass by them. But when they saw Him walking on the sea, they supposed that it was a ghost, and cried out; for they all saw Him and were terrified. But immediately He spoke with them and said to them, "Take courage; it is I, do not be afraid." Then He got into the boat with them, and the wind stopped; and they were utterly astonished, for they had not gained any insight from the incident of the loaves, but their heart was hardened. (Mark 6:45–52, NASB)

Note how the passage says that Jesus saw the disciples straining at the oars because of the storm. You would think Jesus would have leapt to his feet and run out to save them, but then you read *"about the fourth watch of the night,"* which would have been hours later (sometime just before dawn). Jesus decided instead to stay on the mountain and pray until he was good and ready to cross the waters. Then you read, when he finally decided to walk across the sea, *"He intended to pass by them."* Wait! He wasn't even planning on rescuing them! What's going on?

Similarly, in Luke 22:31–32, Jesus tells Simon Peter that Satan has asked to sift him like wheat. Rather than putting a stop to it, he allows it, praying that Peter's faith won't fail. As we see here, Jesus doesn't rush in like Superman to rescue us immediately from our troubles or temptations, but he uses the crises to grow our faith and us. For he knows that as our faith grows, so does our capacity to trust him and experience peace and joy through our troubles.

Can We Still Trust Jesus, No Matter What?

So the question for us then is, can we still trust Jesus and have faith in him even if he doesn't rescue us? Can he be sufficient for us, especially during dark times? Often people will tell me that the times they feel closest to the Lord is when they've come to the end of their rope and are desperate.

The reality is that we often live for self, not God—for our happiness and fulfillment, me-centred versus God-centred—and this is *the* big hindrance to maturity. We all have selfish desires that compete for God's place in our heart and hinder our growth and fruitfulness. It's very easy to be deceived when we want a good thing, even a thing that's scriptural (e.g., a godly husband); these are legitimate desires. But the problem arises when our desires become what we want *most*. When we think we *need* anything other than God himself, we are doomed. We can't serve two masters; it's humanly impossible. So as soon as we can learn to stop wanting what we need more than God, these desires can take their proper place and not be too important in our hearts. They can come down from the thrones of our hearts as idols.

Is it my heart's desire to please God or to please me? We begin to think we need Christ *and* a happy marriage, Christ *and* lots of money. Is it my desire to glorify him or to be happy? If we don't yield and give over our heart's desires to God's authority, someone or something other than God is controlling our lives.

When I see people in my practice and I hear the struggles they have with their spouses or their children, my heart goes out to them because their pain and frustration is very real. It isn't fair that their husbands or wives aren't faithful or godly or considerate or pulling their weight, and they are right to want changes in these areas. But they are deceived if they think they *must* have faithful, godly and considerate spouses or children in order to live as Christ would. These desires then rule their thoughts, actions, emotions and focus, and then they get caught in sinful attitudes and bitterness and fear.

How do we know if we have idols in our hearts? Take them away and watch our reactions. What happens when we don't have power and control, peace and serenity, pleasure or approval, respect or security? What happens when we don't have money, when we're not recognized for our accomplishments, when we're ignored or even humiliated? When we don't get our way? What we fear losing the most will often reveal idols of our heart. When we demand that life be fair, that life be smooth and trouble-free, it holds us back from experiencing the true abundance of the life God gives us.

It's Time to Surrender

Is God enough for you? Are you ready to let go of everything else? Remember, this decision will be *daily*, an ongoing commitment to let nothing interfere in your relationship with God. You will have to keep a short account, because you will continue to wrestle with taking things back and relying on other people or things for your security—I know I do! It will also be a daily decision that you make with your *will*, not your emotions.

Surrendering all to God and contemplating the loss of all else you love can be very frightening. But remember, surrendering it all to God doesn't mean that he is going to take it all away from you. I once struggled with warped thinking, believing that if I let go of my idols I would be giving God license to take every-thing away—how powerful I had been in my own mind! If you believe this, you can be sure it's time to come down a few notches and know that you are letting go of your dependence on these things for your security and well-being. As dif-ficult as this can be, there is unbelievable freedom in this step of surrender. Nothing and no one can take away your God-given and Jesus-purchased *capacity* for peace and joy!

Nothing.

Digging Deep

So, whether you *feel* ready or not, if you've decided it's time, let's begin. Think about all the things, situations and people you hold dear to your heart. List them all in your journal. Nothing about this is easy. But do it praying that God will show you anything else that is occupying a piece of your heart, anything that is interfering in your full dependence on him. Continue to write it all down, one after another as he brings them to mind, and don't stop to consider how dread-fully long that list is. In time, it will grow shorter.

Respond honestly as God shows you your heart, as he convicts you of the parts of your life that are not surrendered to him. Oh, imagine his joy at seeing this willingness to finally engage with his heart and trust him as he deserves, finally receive all his love, which you most assuredly do *not* deserve. Confess it all, all of these idols, and give them to God in faith and complete surrender: your time, your career, your work, your aspirations, your body, your health, your tongue and the words you use, your mind and your intellect, your will and your desires, your emotions, your possessions, your relationships, your reputation, your future, your hopes and dreams, your money, your life.

Ask yourself, "Are there any compartments of my life over which I am reserv-ing the right to exercise control? Have I surrendered all that I am and all that I have to God? Is there any part of myself and my life that I am knowingly holding back from God? Have I released my relationships to him, especially with my spouse and children? Am I trying to control their lives? Is there anyone I love in a way that is not pure? Am I holding on to any friendships or relationships God wants me to relinquish? Do I own anything I wouldn't be willing to part with if God were to take it or ask me to give it up? Am I a wise steward of the resources God has entrusted to me? Am I content with what he has given me? Do I consis-tently seek to know and do the will of God in the practical daily matters of life? Is there anything I know God wants me to do that I have not done or am not doing? Do I become resentful when things don't go my way? Am I stubborn? Demanding? Controlling?"

As God peels apart the parts of your heart that are not fully owned by him, bring each idol to him and confess your refusal to relinquish that part of your life to him. Be honest with him, and trust that he is listening with great love and grace. And then commit (daily) to living fully surrendered to God, giving him full permission to reveal each time you take back a piece of your life. Ask your Father to help you live rooted in the truth that *he is enough.*

SECTION III

Life to the *Full*

"I have come that they may have life, and have it to the full."

John 10:10

CHAPTER 17

Pursuing Your Best Friend

"I have now seen the One who sees me."

Genesis 16:13

During my depression and burnout, when all I wanted to do was retreat and bury myself away from everyone, one of my few links to sanity came through the loving ministrations of a dear friend of mine, Linda. Completely unasked and unexpectedly, she persistently loved me through the darkness with her relentless texts and emails to encourage me, uplifting cards in the mail, small gifts to help me rejuvenate, and her warm hugs and loving presence as she listened to my woes. *She would not let me go, and she would not give up on me.*

And there were other friends: Pamela, who cried with me and listened tenderly as I shared my painful journey with her: *she would not let me do this alone;* Gillian, who gave me perspective and humour and an appreciation of beauty even in sorrow: *she would not let me drown or lose sight of truth;* Wendy, a co-sufferer, who understood my pain as she used her gift of artistry to craft a beautiful necklace for me, a reminder of God as my strong shelter against the rough waters of life: *she would not let me lose hope.* And my husband, Peter, who walked patiently with me. Shouldering more than his fair share of responsibility to give me time to heal, he helped me find the strength to set boundaries and say no to what I needed to turn away from: *he was strong for me when I was weak.* And my mom, Lily, who listened carefully and offered her words of wisdom while wearing out her knees praying intensely for me, crying out to the Lord on my behalf; *she knelt in the gap and petitioned for me.* And my mentor, Adrienne, who knew of my sin and my struggles and yet was grace personified to me and a strong reminder that my Father knows everything and is the Master Storyteller of my life: *she pointed me to my Father's purposes in my story and his sovereignty over every detail.*

At the time I could not understand how Jesus was loving me through my friends and family; I was too immersed in my pain to see that clearly. Depression and darkness has that kind of power. But looking back I see how he used each one to paint a wondrous picture of his love and care, to allow me to experience—and not just "know" in my head—what his friendship with me really means. *He would not let me go, and he would not give up on me. He would not let me do this alone. He would not let me drown in my sorrows or lose sight of truth. He would not let me lose hope. He would be strong for me when I was weak. He would kneel in the gap and petition the Father for me. He would point me to my Father's purposes in my story and his sovereignty over every little detail.*

Inevitably, it was during this desperation that I learned to invest deeply in my friendship with the Lord; it was when I learned to take everything to my Father and learned to really listen to him reassure me with his love and comfort. Through their specific examples, my friends and family taught me to talk honestly to him, listen to him with an open heart, spend time enjoying him and just rest in him. It was during this bleak darkness that I learned to lean on God, that I began to trust in his love and finally understood what it meant to experience true friendship with my Lord. I realize now that this was one of his main purposes for leading me through the winter of my soul. And oh, has it changed my life profoundly.

Jeffrey Imbach says in his book *The Recovery of Love:* "Prayer is essentially the expression of our heart longing for love. It is not so much the listing of our requests but the breathing of our own deepest request, to be united with God as fully as possible."[39] Do you hear that? *To be united with God as fully as possible.* This sounds like *relationship,* doesn't it?

But I've been learning that my Father also longs to be united with me, that his heart's cry is for me to draw close to him—not because he needs it but because he wants it and because I desperately need him. It's because we were created to need him; we were created to be whole in him. But we have to want it. We have to seek it. We have to create space for him.

Busyness Is Earwax

And so we have to intentionally nurture our friendship with the Lord, or it will not flourish. The busyness of life, the din of competing demands, the pressures of responsibilities and the seduction of pleasures all shout loudly to drown out the quiet voice of our Father inviting us to his heart.

In our busyness, we often miss God; the whirlwind of our doing becomes a smoke screen for evasion. Endless busyness is earwax against God's voice and a blindfold to God's presence. God grows mute in the din of our shouting, remote in the blur of our rushing. But stillness reawakens our wonder and attention, and allows us to become freshly present with God, keenly attuned to his speaking.[40]

And so we miss out on a beautiful friendship with our Lord. Oh, we may sense the emptiness in our souls, but what do we do? We fill it with more stuff, more activities, more busyness, more distraction. That is not the way we've been designed to live, and so our joy and peace will always fall short and we will always be hungry: "*Then Jesus declared, 'I am the bread of life. Whoever comes to me will never go hungry, and whoever believes in me will never be thirsty*" (John 6:35).

In our time-starved, increasingly cluttered and hyperactive culture, we have become so conditioned to instant gratification and fast-paced adrenaline-driven activities that we've lost the art of patience; we've forgotten (or never learned) how to cultivate relationships with others; we rarely slow down enough to enjoy the gift of life or savour the beauty of our world and the joys of loving others. And similarly (and possibly as a result as well) we fail to connect with God; we somehow believe that if we spend a quick hour a week at church, somehow our lives will change. People are disconnected and marriages and families are breaking down because no one has time or patience to invest deeply in what really matters, especially in our friendship with our Father.

Manning and Hancock pinpoint the problem:

If someone has promised you can have instant intimacy with God, without a serious investment of time and attention, I can only say you've been sincerely misled. It's the equivalent of a TV dating show where strangers find true love in six episodes. It doesn't happen that way. If their relationship survives to become true love, it happens after the show ends, when they take time to know each other and become truly (and not just physically) intimate.[41]

Instead, it begins with drawing close enough to hear God's whisper, closing the door if necessary to shut out the noise, going outside if that's what it takes to escape the distractions. And it grows as you spend more and more time with him, opening your heart to him and letting him see yours.

The Fully Lived Life

God's a Whisperer

Do you hear that? *It begins with drawing close enough to hear God's whisper.* It also begins with opening up your heart to the possibility of a dynamic relationship with your Father and the hope that he wants to be in communion with you. It doesn't have to be dry, distant, formulaic, legalistic or superficial. Have you *ever* developed a close friendship with anyone without spending time together, sharing your hearts, listening to each other, and enjoying laughter and the pleasure of each other's presence? Why then do we think we must follow some rules, go to church, read our Bible, and pray our list prayers to somehow have an intimate relationship with our Father, that somehow that's how we can *know* him and *be known?*

All those things have defined for us how we know God. But that is not how we know God.

Mark Buchanan says it beautifully in *Hidden in Plain Sight—The Secret of More:*

> God is revealed in Scripture but not bound there. He is a living God. He speaks to us, moves in our midst, surprises us with himself. The heavens cannot contain him, and the whole earth is filled with his glory. To know God, we start with Scripture and return to Scripture, but he also inhabits our praises. He comes close to those contrite in spirit. He rides on the wind. I have watched many people well versed in God's Biblical revelation only really come to *know* him through a worshipful or prayerful encounter with him. They *taste* and *see* that the Lord is good, a truth they never doubted but hadn't experienced.[42]

I know that some of you have been raised with the belief that the only communication we will ever receive from God is through Scripture, and so the idea of having actual conversations with God seems either mildly, strongly, or completely sacrilegious. You may have been taught that God has ceased to communicate with his people other than through his Word, and even if he did speak to you, how could you ever verify whether it is in fact from God? And so you've been advised to stay away from error and adamantly denounce and turn away from all that experiential nonsense. I do realize that many believers in their unbridled enthusiasm have swung too far the other way, and there are truly some bizarre and outlandish things being said and done in the Lord's name—I am certainly not advocating unchecked spiritualism.

But let me gently challenge you, because my heart, and your Father's heart, long for so much more for you. There is a world of joyful communion with the Lord just waiting for you! John Eldredge says in *Walking with God:*

> The prevailing belief is that God speaks to his people *only* through the Bible. And let me make this clear: he does speak to us first and foremost through the Bible... However, many Christians believe that God *only* speaks to us through the Bible. The irony of that belief is that's not what the Bible says...The Bible is filled with stories of God talking to his people. I can hear the objections even now: "But that was different. Those were special people called to special tasks." And we are not special people called to special tasks? I refuse to believe that.[43]

But I never hear from God. Does that mean I'm less spiritual? We are all wired differently, and so our souls will resonate with God in many different ways, from a reverent sense of his presence while worshipping him with music to a joyful awe when we experience a breathtaking sunset we know he meant just for us. Seeing the words of Scripture leap out from the page specifically directed to our current situation and the loving embrace of a friend just when we need it most are ways God speaks to us, if we would just realize it and pay attention, if we would just quiet ourselves enough to listen, watch, pay attention, and open our hearts to our Father's invitation to a life of fullness with him. I will tell you one thing though: it does require us to *want* it and to make space in our lives, our busy schedules and our hearts for him. We have to "*Come near to God and he will come near to [us]*" (James 4:8). It's not so much that God is ever far from our side, but our awareness of his presence greatly increases as we choose to focus on him and draw near to him.

God Longs to Spend Time with Us

If we start with the premise that God *longs* to spend time with us, can you let that truth sink deep into your heart? And would that change your perspective enough to encourage you to make time for your Father? The truth of God's love and longing for us is woven throughout all of Scripture, and his actions since the beginning of time continue to echo that truth.

Lest you measure your relationship with God based on the number of times he speaks to you, please hear me: hearing God speak to you happens more as you become aware of it—but focus on doing life with God and inviting him into the inner recesses of your heart, all the good, the bad and the ugly, and trust that he is there, interested in you and willing and speaking to you as your heart is made ready to hear. Prepare your heart to hear by presenting yourself to him, regardless of the outcome. It's also about savouring God like a delicious feast, taking time to enjoy all the subtleties of his flavours. Sometimes it's just about hanging out with your Father for the experience of being together without any deep dialogue.

A number of years ago, during the height of my religiosity and performance-based Christianity, feeling very dispirited and confused, I came upon a book called *The Pursuit of Holiness* by Jerry Bridges (in my works-based focus, I thought for sure this book would give me the secret formula for being "holy"), and I learned that my focus was all wrong.[44] Rather than focusing on *obeying* God and on my ability to be good, I was to focus on *loving* God, and as I grew to love him more and more, obedience would be a natural outflow of that love.

When I used to read in John 14:15 the words "*If you love Me, you will keep My commandments*" (NASB), I thought I had to *prove* that I loved Jesus by obeying him. In actuality, if I fall in love with Jesus with all my heart, soul and mind, then I will naturally obey him, not as a duty but as a *delight*. If I draw near to the Lord in intimacy, hungry and passionate for him, I will choose not to sin, because I don't want to break my fellowship with him. Intimacy with God is truly the only way to break the power of sin in my life. God's Word is no longer simply a *restraint* with all its rules, but it's become my *delight*.

Being Alone with Our Best Friend

There is no formula for developing a close friendship with our Lord, but being alone with our Father moves us from head knowledge of his love for us to real and experienced *felt* knowledge. It takes us from dry theology to a knowing deep in our soul.

And time alone with our Father is so worth it—it is life-giving, life-illuminating and life-changing. Manning and Hancock remind us, "Our longing to know who we truly are will never be satisfied until we embrace solitude—not loneliness, that's a different thing—but genuine solitude where we discover that we are Totally Loved by God."[45] No one can communicate that to us but the One who knows us completely and loves us without reservation. Until you spend time alone with God, you won't experience this truth for yourself. And he does that in private, just you and your best friend alone. Quiet yourself for a moment, and I promise you, God will meet you there.

You hear that? *God will meet you there.* This is key to living your life as God created you: if you were looking for the secret to happiness or the key to eternal youth, this is it. This is the true full life, something we all so desperately need

154

but so often miss in our frantic pursuit of all the substitutes. Without time alone with God,

> Our controlled frenzy creates the illusion of a well-ordered existence. We move from crisis to crisis, responding to the urgent and neglecting the essential. We will perform all the gestures and actions identified as human, but we resemble people carried along on the mechanical sidewalk at an airport. *The fire in the belly dies. We no longer hear…"the inward music" of our belovedness.*[46] (emphasis mine)

I don't want the "fire in my belly" to die. I want to live my life to the full, rooted in the truth of who I am and the complete truth of my belovedness. So what does all this mean for you? Patience, my friend, and persistence. Consider your friendship with your Father like a fine wine to be slowly cultivated and then enjoyed. Remember that this will take time and much practice.

Knowing Your Father

I have discovered four keys to growing intimacy with my Father:

Knowing God involves talking with and listening to God, not just going to him with a long laundry list of all that you want him to do for you. If you have ever fallen in love, remember those days when all you wanted to do was see that person and spend time with them talking and getting to know them? That's what God wants you to do with him, not talking superficially but sharing your true heart with him and seeking out his. There are many wonderful resources that teach the ancient spiritual disciplines that draw believers into the presence of God.[47] The key aspect is a deliberate focus on the Lord and spending time in his presence and in his Word.

Knowing God involves learning to discern his voice. Listening is hard work, and it's even harder to listen to God. There are so many competing voices of the world, our flesh and Satan, and they are always louder. Recognize some of these: voice of criticism, voice of self-righteousness, voice of self-pity, voice of self-indulgence. That is not the voice of your Father. How often do you listen to the grating and demeaning voices in your head? How often have you mistakenly thought that it's God beating you up for messing up yet again?

What does God's voice sound like? You will know it when you hear it. And you will hear it when you listen for it and talk with him. It has several characteristics.

It is gentle, quiet and deeply internal; it's never threatening, demanding, strident, or intimidating. It is always consistent with Scripture, always grace-filled and loving. When he speaks truth, it's convicting, never condemning. He's usually focused on changing us, not on urging us to change others. Grounded in truth and hope, not in past negative experiences, his counsel is simple and direct rather than complicated and impractical, often in the ordinary and mundane things of life rather than the spectacular.

The effect of an encounter with God is more hope, empathy and compassion for others and a greater sense of peace, even when circumstances don't change.

Knowing God involves valuing what he says over how you feel. If we don't believe what he says, we can never experience God in a deeper way. What you believe in your heart is how you'll live. I have seen this countless times in my office and my own life. There is even scientific evidence that if you believe you are a failure at something, you *will* under-perform and eventually fail. Commit to God to believe in his words. We are blessed with times when we really *feel* close to God and sense his presence, but the real test of our relationship with God is continuing to draw close to him even when we don't *feel* close to him. It's not in the mountaintop experiences that our true faith is seen but in the daily experiences of life.

Knowing God intimately must include obeying him. God desires that we love and trust him and willingly yield our will to him. Would you feel close to someone who didn't respect what you said and didn't trust you? God *will not* disclose himself to those who aren't interested in the things he's interested in or who aren't willing to trust and follow him.

Do you know how much God truly loves you? Do you comprehend the depth of his mercy and compassion for you? Think of it: the God of creation, who spoke this world into being, who made you exactly as he planned you to be, loves you beyond comprehension, and as a measure of his love he gave himself to you. Beyond all that he *does* for us, remember that he gives *himself* to us in love and longs for us to reciprocate.

"I Have All the Time in the World for You"

I'll close this chapter by sharing one of my recent experiences in my quiet time with the Lord that I pray will be an encouragement to you. Let our Father's words resonate in your heart as a message to *you:*

"Rest in me, my child. I have all the time in the world for you. Make time for Me and you will not be disappointed. Only I can fill the hunger in your soul.

Come, just enjoy me. Let's just be together—no goals, no agendas, nothing to be accomplished—other than I'm teaching you how to be in a love relationship with me. Draw close to me and I promise we will grow together. You will come to know my heart more and more and my will for your life. This is my will for you—to spend time with me, knowing my love for you, worshipping me and spending your life to bring me glory. The more you spend time with me, the more your heart and thoughts will be opened to me and the more you will become the person I've created you to be.

But you don't have to draw apart always in silence and solitude. Invite me into your daily life, into all the minutiae of your life—let's do life together. I am always with you and in your heart. My words to you will resonate in your heart because I am teaching you to trust your heart. All of our time together is about heart connection, whether words are exchanged or not. Don't always look for the mountaintop experience and lose sight of our relationship and our daily walk together. What may not seem deep and meaningful is another day building our relationship— which is deep and meaningful and miraculous. Enjoy the gift of our intimacy—that is the purpose of our time together.

When I choose, there will be times when I will speak and you will know it's from Me.

Keep your heart and your mind turned toward me, consult me on all things and then heed what I say. It's simple! Remember, I love being with you. Let my love warm your heart. Enjoy me, my child, savour me and my love for you."

Pause and ponder the reminder of the simplicity of a life turned to your Father. In focusing on your friendship with God, don't worry about trying to figure out the hows and what you're supposed to do. Don't beat yourself up for doing it wrong, for not figuring it out. That is not what your Father wants. He wants you to simply present yourself to him and quiet your mind and heart—just be with your Father. Do what Mark Buchanan urges us to do: "Cease from what is necessary. Embrace that which gives life."[48]

Embrace that which gives life. Embrace the gift your Father is offering you— a *full* life with him. Allow yourself to pause long enough in your busy schedule to notice the longing in your heart. Is deep calling out to deep in your soul?

Digging Deep

If that isn't what you're currently experiencing, ask yourself, What is preventing me from pursuing a friendship with God with all my heart? Ask yourself,

Do I enjoy my time with God? Do I wish for more of it? Or does it often feel like a duty? Is God's Word shaping me? Or am I mostly influenced by other things—work, moods, circumstances, others?

If spending time with your Father in silence and solitude is a foreign activity for you, don't beat yourself up for feeling uncomfortable. This is not about being more "spiritual." And don't let *my* experiences dictate what yours should be like. We are all wired differently, so consider this a time of experimenting. My longing for you—your Father's longing for you—is that you draw closer to him. No agenda. No "shoulds." Just being together.

Start small. Begin by setting aside five minutes to quiet yourself before God. Pick a place that fills you with peace, whether it's outside sitting in your garden with a cup of tea or in a quiet place hidden somewhere in your home. Sit in your car if you have to! It doesn't matter where, as long as you can be alone and undisturbed. Unplug yourself from the Internet, cellphone, etc. Sit quietly before God. There's no need to say anything to him or do to anything. When I first started practicing silence and solitude, I found it helpful to focus on a phrase that helped me stay centred on God; otherwise my busy mind would distract me into a thousand different directions. I experimented with various phrases like "Lord, I long for you" and "More of you, less of me."

If you get distracted, don't worry about it. This is about practicing the art of quieting yourself before the Lord, and it will take time. *Just don't give up.* Over time, you can experiment with longer periods of time with God, including journaling. Because I am very verbal, I like writing my thoughts to God. I then ask him to share his heart for me and wait. I then let my pen capture the thoughts that come to mind. I trust the Spirit of God to guide my words as I "hear" him, but I also know that I have to prayerfully test the words and make sure that nothing I am hearing is inconsistent with God's truth as revealed in his Word. And I filter it through some of the guidelines I shared previously.

As you spend more and more time with him, you will learn to quickly recognize his voice and experience his presence more deeply in your everyday life. You will feel him as a *knowing* deep in your spirit.

I promise you, you will never regret the time you spend with your Father.

CHAPTER 18

Listening to Your Heart

I run in the path of your commandments, for you have set my heart free.

Psalm 119:32, WEB

Gina sat at the edge of the chair, tears spilling down her lovely face as she shook her head. Unable to answer my question of what she wanted to do after she finished school, she was hopeless and despondent. She hated her university courses, and she was desperately unhappy with her life. She was struggling with depression and anxiety, but she didn't know why. After years of following the lead of others, including her harsh, domineering mother and the authoritarian, legalistic leaders in her church, Gina had no voice. She had no opinions, thoughts or choices that weren't rooted in what someone else wanted for her.

What she did have of her own was emotions. And mostly what she felt was a crushing sense of self-hatred mingled with dark thoughts of suicide—a tempting end to her miserable existence.

I felt an aching sadness looking at Gina, so beautiful in all of her unrealized potential but unable to blossom because she was raised in the dark shadow of her family's punitive control. Had she been given the life-giving sunlight of nurturing love, she might have been allowed to develop as her Father had designed. Now all that could help her was healing in a safe relationship, one that offered her acceptance, grace and understanding, with someone who wouldn't give her answers but would gently guide her to her own heart and voice.

It wasn't until months later, after Gina was able to process through her wounds and wrestle through her painful sense of isolation and abandonment by her Father, that she was finally able to begin to speak. Oh, the sacred beauty of the moment when she began to know her own heart and began to see who she was as her Father's beloved! The moment when she began to speak up and declare her own thoughts, opinions and desires was a moment that I will always remember and cherish.

Like a butterfly unfurling its delicate wings for the first time, Gina began to listen to her heart and speak words of hope, desires and yearning that were long buried in her heart by her Father, her treasure to be discovered, pursued and savoured. Beyond discovering she was a child of God and his great love for her, the discovery of her own unique calling and her own God-given voice was the point at which her life began to finally take shape in a way that God had willed it to be.

But it didn't come without a cost. As she began to listen to her heart, she had to work hard to ignore the competing demands of others, and so there were many setbacks. As she began to speak up, she had to experience the rejection and condemnation of her family and friends, and so she had to find new friends who were safe for her and would accept her as she was. And as she began to dream about a life lived fully for God as he created her to be, she had to risk hugely and step outside her comfort zone. But because she was following the roadmap her Father had implanted in her heart—the treasure map he meant for her to discover—she was filled with light and hope and joy. And having had her heart set free by her Father, she was ready to run in the path of his commands.

The Springs of Life

Does Gina's story stir anything in your heart? Have you been feeling trapped and longing to break free? To live life to the full? Do you wonder why you seem to continually face drudgery and weariness in your life? The Bible says that out of your heart *flow* the springs of life (Proverbs 4:23), and so if you're ignoring your heart, your life isn't flowing in the way God designed it to. Curtis and Eldredge say it well in *The Sacred Romance:* "Life teaches us very early on to ignore our desires…We learn to offer only those parts of us that are approved, living out a careful performance to gain acceptance. [And so] we divorce ourselves from our heart and live a double life."[49]

That was true for me. For so long, I listened to others and lived out of rigid and demanding scripts they wrote for me. I learned to be responsible, disciplined, faithful, diligent and dutiful. Not bad things at all, mind you, but something seemed to be missing. I didn't quite understand what it was until I read *Dare to Desire* by John Eldredge. My rusty heart began to stir in longing as I read, "Don't ask yourself what the world needs. Ask yourself what makes you come alive, and go do that, because what the world needs is people who have come alive."[50]

To "come alive" was so opposite to how I was feeling at the time, I almost didn't know how to respond. What does it mean to come alive? And how could I do that? And wasn't following my heart selfish? I had so many responsibilities; how could I possibly lay them down to discover and follow my heart's desires? On and on I wrestled—on the one hand, I was beginning to feel a longing to pursue my heart's desires, while on the other I butted up against a lifetime of religious teaching about the "shoulds" and the "responsibilities of life" as a Christ-follower.

Resisting and sceptical, yet still intrigued, I began to read John Eldredge's earlier book, *Desire*. And this was some of what I read:

I believe desire is a gift from God. After all, the psalms say things like, "May he give you the desire of your heart" (20:4); and "Praise the Lord, O my soul…who satisfies your desires with good things so that your youth is renewed like the eagle's" (103:5); and "You open your hand and satisfy the desire of every living thing" (145:16). Clearly, God is not opposed to desire. Far from it. He gives us a heart that desires deeply, and he uses those desires to draw us to himself, and to the life he created us to live. What we need to learn is how to listen to desire, how to *interpret* it. Desire is speaking to us, all the time. It is one of the deepest voices of the heart. A voice many of us have never been taught to understand.[51]

And as I read, I began to understand that what he meant by "heart" was much more than just feelings, that my "heart" was based on more than my fickle emotions, which could be as changeable as the weather. Instead, he meant it to encompass the deepest and truest me—the person I was meant to be *if life had gone the way it was meant to go.* I'd soon find that Manning and Hancock agreed: "The heart is the deepest essence of a person. It symbolizes what's at our core. The heart of the matter is that we can know and be known only through revealing what's in our heart."[52]

Buried Treasures

Reading Eldredge's words, I realized that I had buried my desires, my heart, and in so doing had allowed others' demands to dictate the choices of my life. And as my heart began to stir at his words, I started to journal:

I am so tired of playing it safe. I long to live with passion and joy, to live life fully and truly as an adventure. I've been so afraid of coming across as prideful and too concerned with being a "sanctified" Christian that I haven't allowed myself to fully dream. Papa, are you awakening the longings in my soul?

161

As I journalled, I began to feel such a welling over of sadness and grief in my heart that I began to weep.

Why am I so sad? What is this triggering in me?

I realized I was experiencing the desolation of a lifetime of putting aside my own desires and dreams to please others. Lest that sound noble and self-sacrificing, let me quickly add that part of my sorrow stemmed from the realization that my choice to live this way came out of a bottomless hunger and emptiness, a fear of losing the "love" of others, and a choice to chase the phantom of others' approval in a futile attempt to shore up the shaky foundations of my sense of worth.

As I cried, I began to feel a burgeoning lightness in my spirit as I started to accept that maybe, just maybe, God had more in mind for me than a life of drudgery and duty and that he *was* urging me to listen to my heart. They weren't just pretty words dreamt up by my life coach or a "selfish" thought that came out of my sinful heart. Maybe, just maybe, the encouragement was coming from my Father, inviting me into a life of fullness with him.

The Awakening of Our Desires

Does it sound impossible that God might be interested in our desires, our heart longings? Do my words seem almost irreverent with what you've been taught? I deeply believe that the heart has gotten a bad rap in some Christian circles. As I shared in chapter 12 on emotions, there is fear in many of us that if we "give in" to our emotions, we are giving in to our sinful nature. For some reason, we equate our sins with our emotions, and so we try instead to be stoic and controlled.

We lose sight of the fullness of who we're made to be in the image of our Father. We forget about the images of King David dancing down the street, so filled with joy in the Lord he could not contain himself. Think of that. We forget about Jesus' joy and his deep sadness as he faced the agony of the cross. We ignore the many stories in the Bible of people following their hearts and living fully for God—raw, real, emotional and impassioned. And so I ask you: in our buttoned-down rational life, are we *really* living life as God meant us to?

Above all, the Christian life is the life of the heart. It can't be managed by simply following a set of rules or principles. It's not just about ethics or a moral code. When Jesus was asked about the secret of real life, he posed a question in return: "*What is written in the Law? How do you read it?*" The man who asked the question answered, "'*Love the Lord your God with all your heart and with all your* *soul and with all your strength and with all your mind'; and, 'love your neighbor as yourself.'" "'You have answered correctly,' Jesus replied. 'Do this and **you will live**"* (Luke 10: 26–28, emphasis mine).

Do you hear that? Love God and love others, and *you will live.* Jesus came to set us free to love God and others with our whole hearts. Paul reminds us in 1 Corinthians 13:1–3 (NLT):

> *If I could speak all the languages of earth and of angels, but didn't love others, I would only be a noisy gong or a clanging cymbal. If I had the gift of prophecy, and if I understood all of God's secret plans and possessed all knowledge, and if I had such faith that I could move mountains, but didn't love others, I would be nothing. If I gave everything I have to the poor and even sacrificed my body, I could boast about it; but if I didn't love others, I would have gained nothing.*

When we ignore this heart aspect of our faith and try to live out our religion only as correct doctrine, our passion is crippled and we miss out on the full life God intended for us.

Do you hear that? *Our passion is crippled.* Not only are we missing out on the fullness of life, but we're not living in God's will, the way he designed us to exist. John Eldredge reminds us, "We don't need more facts, and we certainly don't need more things to do. We need *Life,* and we've been looking for it ever since we lost Paradise. Jesus appeals to our desire because he came to speak to it."[53] He goes on to warn us that "when we abandon desire, we no longer hear or understand what [Jesus] is saying."[54] We become deaf to our Father's voice when we turn away from our hearts.

When the prophet Samuel was a young boy, he heard the voice of God calling to him in the night. Eli told him how to respond, and so Samuel discovered it was God calling. Rather than ignoring the voice or criticizing it, Samuel learned to listen. Having been so long out of touch with our deepest longings in our modern, pragmatic world, we don't understand that God is speaking to our hearts. But the heart is central and in fact is addressed in the Bible more than believing, obeying, or serving, even more than money and worship. "*For the eyes of the LORD range throughout the earth to strengthen those whose hearts are fully committed to him*" (2 Chronicles 16:9).

The Cost of Awakening Our Hearts

Paying attention to our hearts doesn't come without a significant cost—and this may be why so many are afraid. Awakening our hearts opens us up to experience pain and suffering and can create profound vulnerability *feeling* what most prefer to avoid:

> To want is to suffer; the word *passion* means to suffer. This is why many Christians are reluctant to listen to their hearts: they know that their dullness is keeping them from feeling the pain of life. Many of us have chosen simply not to want so much; it's safer that way. It's also godless. That's stoicism, not Christianity. Sanctification is an awakening, the rousing of our souls from the dead sleep of sin into the fullness of their capacity for life.[55]

I know that the fear of disappointment—having my hopes and desires dashed ruthlessly by a capricious God who gives and takes away—has paralyzed me. Better not to hope and want than to experience the shattering pain of disappointment. Better to err on the safe side, ignore my heart, and avoid the possibility of lost dreams and, even worse, the possibility of disappointing God and, honestly, others. I focused on what others wanted, and on what I *made believe* God wanted, so that I wouldn't lose approval, a fate worse than death.

But my Father, in his great love and full understanding of what I needed, taught me to listen to my heart, not only to free me from needing approval, but so I could be myself. And as I persisted wrestling with grief over losing sight of my heart, I wrote in my journal:

> I am starting to realize that sadness plays an important part in our life because it highlights what we are missing, what we are deeply yearning and longing for to the core of our being—it points us to heaven, for the life we were created for. My sadness has been to be deeply known and loved and to find a place of deep significance and value. Because what I long for is impossible this side of heaven—at least in its complete fruition—I experience sadness. I know that I have exhausted myself chasing something I was unable to achieve because it's not something I'm meant to chase. I am meant to long for and be in touch with my desires so I can find hope of our eternal future—it also draws me to the only One who can satisfy all my longings. To you, Papa. Because you ARE the Promised Land. You are heaven on earth, you are the source for all love and joy and purpose and pleasure.

And this is what my Father had to say to me:

"The path I have put you on is to revel in me, to taste and see that I am good. I want you to break free from the 'shoulds' of life. I want you to live life fully and deeply, with joy and laughter. Enjoy life and stop worrying about the future. Trust your heart and me in it. Listen to your heart, listen to my voice in your heart, follow it and trust me with the outcome. If you follow your heart guided by me, you will fulfill your calling and you will live the abundant life I have promised you.

Finding Your Voice ·

Having a voice is God's will for us. But all too often, we seek our voice amidst the cacophony of others, the steady roar of the world. We think if we shout louder or speak longer, maybe pontificate more astutely or perform better, then we'll be heard—somehow it will prove our voice. If we can somehow flag down the attention of others, our voice will matter.

Years ago when I first started working, a co-worker told a friend she hated listening to me speak, that my voice was "shrill." I was horribly offended and set about avoiding this nasty co-worker who had judged me so unfairly. Looking back, I know what she meant. I was so set on proving myself and being heard, I spoke aggressively and loudly over others, talking more than listening.

For years, I wanted to write. It was a dream of mine since I was a young child, but I ended up going down a different road and putting the dream aside. Years later, I began writing but God showed me I was motivated by my need to feel important, rooted in my childhood insecurities. The pain of feeling stuck in silence, of being ignored, is a desperate neediness, and my writing would have been compromised. And so he asked me to give him my dream of writing. Reluctantly, painfully and only after wrestling, I did what I knew was best. I didn't know it then, but God wanted to do much more work in my heart and to teach me things about him and about myself.

As the words pour forth today, I understand now that he had a plan. Reviewing my journal entries and remembering coming through the Land of the Unknown, I can see now what I didn't realize back then. Oh, to see the hand of God all through my life, even the times in the desert, the times when he seemed so silent!

But so that I would not swing too far astray the other way, spending only time listening to my heart, my Father gently reminded me to stay rooted in Scripture and to guard my heart with his truths so that my emotions don't lead me astray. Anchored by his words through Scripture, learning to trust his voice in my heart that was personal to me, that was what he was teaching me. God would grow me and stretch my faith *through* my dreams, not *in spite* of them. The *content* of my life and the actual *events* of my life aren't the issue—it's what my Father does with them, how he uses *everything* for his good purposes.

In finding my voice I needed to stop being so afraid of my heart. And if I could, I could begin to live passionately and fully for Christ.

An Encouragement from Your Father

As I close this chapter, I want to reprint here a note I received from a dear friend of mine while deep in the Land of the Unknown, struggling to break free to trust the heart of my Father. As you read his note, may his words greatly encourage you as they did for me that morning that I desperately needed to hear from the Lord:

Reading this morning in Psalm 20:3–5 your name jumped to mind as I read this passage...

May he remember all your sacrifices and accept your burnt offerings. May he give you the desire of your heart and make all your plans succeed. May we shout for joy over your victory and lift up our banners in the name of our God. May the LORD grant all your requests.

- He does remember all your sacrifices...
- He has accepted your offerings and is very pleased...
- He will give you the desires of your heart...
- He will make your plans succeed...
- There will be shouts of joy and partying as your requests are met...

Have a day of complete rest in him.

Digging Deep

If you had permission to do what you really want to do, what would you do? If you could change anything in your life, what would it be? Don't ask or think about *how* right now; just listen to your heart. What is written in your heart? What makes you come alive? What—or who—is killing your heart right now in your life?

What is preventing you from listening to your heart? Is it your history, bad theology, your fears, lies that you have believed about yourself and God?

Take some time right now to ask your Father to show you *his* heart for you and then to begin to show you your own heart. Ask him to show you the lies that are preventing you from breaking free, and then commit your heart to him—your emotions, your dreams, your longings, your desires, your voice.

If you don't know what's in your heart right now, don't worry. Believe that God has planted dreams in your that he intends to fulfill, and choose to keep your heart open to him. Do the work outlined in previous chapters to root out anything that is preventing you from knowing your heart—do it over and over as many times as needed to free your heart.

CHAPTER 19

Sinning Boldly

For it is by grace you have been saved, through faith—and this is not from yourselves, it is the gift of God—not by works, so that no one can boast.

Ephesians 2:8–9

I surveyed my outfit one last time before donning the princess sunglasses. Feather boa—*check,* tiara—*check,* pink pajamas—*check.* Smirking at myself in the mirror, I couldn't believe how far I'd come. My heart was pounding as I danced around in my pink ballet slippers, impatient to get the party started. Finally, I was going to let loose. I was attending a princess pajama party at a women's conference, after spending the earlier part of the day learning to embrace my power as a female and my freedom to be fully me (without going into details, let's just say it involved burlesque dancing and high heels).

Several hours later, I was on an adrenaline high, having danced non-stop. Were those really my hips swivelling so freely? Were those really my arms thrust high in triumph above my head as I danced? Was that really me, drawing woman after woman onto the dance floor—inviting them to experience their freedom too? Oh, the unbelievable joy of expressing myself physically without worrying about what others thought. I thumbed my nose at all the Pharisees in my head. *No more.* Shedding the religious shackles of my youth, I chose to step boldly into celebrating the beautiful, vibrant woman God had created me to be.

The interesting aspect about that evening was that I not only danced with abandon, but I also engaged many women in conversation—freely and openly sharing my heart. As I stepped boldly into my freedom, I became more of a light, attracting person after person who was able to relax into who they were as they experienced my acceptance of them and my authenticity. Isn't that how we're meant to connect with one another?

Research shows the benefits of dancing—beyond simply the exercise aspect of it. Dancing is known to ward off dementia by a whopping 76 percent—which most physical activity does not. The tango has been shown to improve mobility for those with Parkinson's disease. Dancing is linked to psychological well-being—just one lively dance session can stave off depression more than vigorous exercise. Getting jiggy with others also leads to less stress and stronger social bonds. And swinging your hips regularly in dance? It's been linked to better health in women's reproductive organs.

I picture King David dancing with abandon; I picture Jesus attending a wedding where wine was served (surely there was dancing there). Oh, and heaven? *"The young women will **dance for joy**, and the men—old and young—will join in the celebration"* (Jeremiah 31:13, NLT, emphasis mine).

Yet I grew up—as many of you may have—during a time when dancing was frowned upon. And certainly, secular music would lead us down a life of sin. Playing cards were an instrument of the devil.

In our pursuit of holiness, where did we go wrong?

Spiritual Freedom

Martin Luther is famous for his dictum *Sola fide*, "by faith alone." Beyond the gift of salvation that comes to us by faith alone, he also believed—after a time of intense struggle with feelings of sinful worthlessness—that our capacity to live the Christian life is by faith alone and not by our works. It is in light of this belief that he penned in a letter to his friend Philip Melanchthon on August 1, 1521, "Be a sinner and sin boldly." That led to his famous phrase "sin boldly," for which he has been much criticized.

Of course, Luther's intent is not conveyed at all in the quote. The full quote from Luther to Melanchthon reads:

> If you are a preacher of mercy, do not preach an imaginary but the true mercy. If the mercy is true, you must therefore bear the true, not an imaginary sin. God does not save those who are only imaginary sinners. Be a sinner and let your sins be strong [sin boldly], but let your trust in Christ be stronger, and rejoice in Christ who is the victor over sin, death, and the world. We will commit sins while we are here, for this life is not a place where justice resides. We, however, says Peter [2 Peter 3:13] are looking forward to a new heaven and a new earth where justice will reign.[56]

The idea was that God's grace is so powerful, it finally defeats sin altogether. According to Luther, this is something to be greatly celebrated because we no longer need to feel paralyzed by our human inability to fight sin on our own.

In reaction to his radical statements, Luther's opponents said that his doctrine of salvation by grace alone apart from our own righteous deeds was a "license to sin."

Yet Luther was not the enemy of virtue his critics made him out to be. He didn't dismiss the importance of good works—he simply wanted to put them in their rightful place. Here, for example, is one of his reflections on the relationship between faith and works:

> Christ teaches us it's not enough to praise faith and Christ, but we also need to produce Christian fruit. For where the fruits aren't evident, or where their opposite appears, Christ is certainly not present….But some will object, "doesn't faith justify and save us without works?" Yes, that's true. But where's your faith? How does it show itself? Faith must never be useless, deaf, dead, or in a state of decay. But it must be a living tree that bursts forth with fruit. That's the difference between genuine faith and false faith. Where there is true faith, it will show itself in a person's life.[57]

He also wrote, "We should always remember that where there is no faith, there can be no good works, and where there are no good works, there is no faith. Therefore, we must keep faith and good works connected. The entire Christian life is embodied by both."[58]

Ironically, Luther was not the first person to be accused of giving license to sin. This is an issue that stirs up deep spiritual unrest for many people. Almost 1,500 years earlier Paul wrote, "*We…know that a person is not justified by the works of the law, but by faith in Jesus Christ*" (Galatians 2:15–16). Paul wrote these words to the churches of Galatia at a time when Jewish teachers were coming from Jerusalem to bring Christian converts under the law of Moses, requiring all believers to be circumcised and obey the law of Moses in order to be right with God. This would in effect destroy Paul's message of good news in Christ:

> *Saving is all his idea, and all his work. All we do is trust him enough to let him do it. It's God's gift from start to finish! We don't play the major role. If we did, we'd probably go around bragging that we'd done the whole thing! No, we neither make nor save ourselves. God does both the making and saving.* (Ephesians 2:8–9, MSG)

Paul was accused by some early Christians of giving a "license to sin" because of his teaching of salvation by faith alone apart from earning salvation through good works.

By Faith Alone

So why did God include these Scriptures for us? In his great love for us—knowing our human tendency towards wanting to earn our way and the bondage that comes through our impossible battle with sin—he knew that we needed this important, life-changing truth. He gave us the key to freedom in Christ Jesus: by faith alone, not by our own works or effort. Our works are *fruits* of our faith and empowered solely by the Holy Spirit in us, not a *means* to personal holiness.

For me, now middle-aged and a Christian for more than four decades, I've ridden the "sin-confess-sin-confess" express train to condemnation plenty of times. And I have come to realize that we humans were simply not created with the capacity to fight sin on our own. There's no "sin-fighting gene" that comes as part of the package. No matter my heart's desire to obey God, I will still fail if I try to battle sin in my own strength.

Paul expands on this human frailty in Romans 7:17–25 (MSG):

But I need something more! For if I know the law but still can't keep it, and if the power of sin within me keeps sabotaging my best intentions, I obviously need help! I realize that I don't have what it takes. I can will it, but I can't do it...Something has gone wrong deep within me and gets the better of me every time...Is there no one who can do anything for me? Isn't that the real question? The answer, thank God, is that Jesus Christ can and does.

Do What Needs Doing

The day that I read Martin Luther's quote "Sin boldly" was a turning point for me; it began to breathe life into the wintery dryness of my soul. In penning his thoughts on grace, he was expressing well the human condition—by the very act of getting out of bed this morning, by my very nature as a fallen human being, by my awakening in this sin-wracked world of ours, I was guaranteeing that there would be some no-good outcome. Whether by doing something I shouldn't or neglecting something I should, whether intending good but hurting or offending someone or being blind to hidden motivations, there is no waking up without some sort of falling out somewhere. My decision to stop and help a neighbour means I don't have time to help my kids with their homework. My decision to go to church means I'm not available for that desperate phone call from my friend.

Mark Buchanan says it well in *Hidden in Plain Sight:* "If every act, intended for the best of ends, is sinful anyhow, then sin boldly. Don't anguish over every last little thing. Do what needs doing and leave the outcome to God."[59] This really struck me—how often I shrink back from something or chastise myself for wanting something just because I am so aware of the possible negative fallout, the great spectre of sin hanging over me.

But God is greater than any sin. He has redeemed me and forgiven me of *all* sin. The enemy uses this fear to hold me back from being honest with what I really want or pursuing it, for fear of appearing prideful or vain. I think actually that's the biggest thing holding me back: the question of what I will look like to other Christians and to God. I'm learning to put aside the opinion of others and not let my fear of their disapproval hamper me from doing what I want. And I'm learning that God's opinion of me is as his beloved. What I want or don't want, what I do or don't do, is irrelevant to his view of me. I can't earn his approval, and I can't lose his positive regard for me. He already *knows* what my heart wants. He knows all of the mixed motivations in my heart—the good, the bad and the ugly.

How Often Have We Played It Safe?

Beyond the growing freedom that I felt with Martin Luther's statement, I also began to feel sadness for how I've lived in fear and the many lost opportunities to see the glory of God in my life.

And this is where we come to the point: in our desire to avoid sin, how often have we played it safe? I know I have. In my struggle to always do the right thing I have coloured too carefully within the prescribed lines and missed out on the enormity of God's incredible and outrageous plans for and through my life.

I had a conversation recently with a good friend. He was struggling with doing the "right thing" in a difficult situation with a family member. But in our conversations, it became evident that he was ruled by the fear of doing the "wrong" thing, so he became paralyzed and unable to act. His inaction only escalated the situation, and he couldn't see God at work in it. He was playing it too safe in his desire to be a good Christian.

In light of this truth, the story of the talents in Matthew 25:24–30 is even more poignant and convicting:

The Fully Lived Life

"'Master, I know you have high standards and hate careless ways, that you demand the best and make no allowances for error. I was afraid I might disappoint you, so I found a good hiding place and secured your money. Here it is, safe and sound down to the last cent.' The master was furious. 'That's a terrible way to live! It's criminal to live cautiously like that! If you knew I was after the best, why did you do less than the least? The least you could have done would have been to invest the sum with the bankers, where at least I would have gotten a little interest. Take the thousand and give it to the one who risked the most. And get rid of this "play-it-safe" who won't go out on a limb. Throw him out into utter darkness.'" (MSG)

I played it safe; I was afraid to disappoint God, so I buried my talents. Having seen God as a harsh taskmaster with impossible standards for much of my life, I lived cautiously. I did what I *thought* he wanted me to do, what I saw others expected or did in similar situations. Since I didn't truly trust God and only feared his anger, I couldn't take risks to speak or act boldly. Fearful of sinning, I became black and white in my thinking, following the rules carefully and scrutinizing God's Word so I could safely avoid his disapproval and anger.

If I reused a stamp that didn't get stamped by the post office, was I stealing? If I drove more than five kilometres over the speed limit, was I breaking the law? I couldn't obey the whisper in my spirit to do that crazy thing for God, for what if I heard him wrong? What if I messed up everything too badly? And so my life became a monotony of rules and duty, parched and shrivelled. And in all of this, I thought for sure if I did what I *really* wanted, I was simply being sinful, selfish, unholy and irresponsible, so I needed to "suck it up."

Into the desert of my life came the stream of life through Luther's words— if I truly accept that God loves me, that I'm covered by his grace, and that in Jesus God sees me as *"holy and blameless"* (Ephesians 1:4); if I accept that he foreknew all of my sins, past, present and future, and in that reality God chose to make me a daughter of his; if I accept that God knows that I'm a sinner yet sees me only as a saint, then the whole trajectory of my life changes.

I can choose to live boldly, trusting him in the outcome—that he will use it for good, even if I mess up very badly (Romans 8:28). I can choose to see life as an adventure with my Father, a wild roller coaster of a life, where there will be many ups and downs, many heartaches and regrets, yet, oh, the joy! If I can accept that he has created me to live life fully, to do the very work that he has prepared for me to do, work that will only bear fruit if it comes through him and by him and for him, work that he has uniquely shaped me to do with passion, joy and purpose, then what do I have to lose?

And more astoundingly, the more I live life boldly—the way he means me to—the more I draw closer to my Father in dependence, gratitude and intimacy. *This* is the full life that he promised us. This is how to live freely in the love and care of our Father.

Don't Be Afraid of Life

God spoke to me, and his words resonated in my soul to live *free* and confidently in his love:

"Oh, how I love you, my child. You're learning to stop fretting so much, to stop trying to be the 'perfect' Christian in your own strength, to accept that you cannot do it on your own, that without me, you can do nothing. You will never have a full understanding of yourself and your motivations this side of heaven—stop with the self-examination—always searching your own heart for sin—and instead open your heart to my light. Open your life to being examined by me—not for me to nitpick, nag, criticize and judge—but for me to convict, change, challenge and show you. Leave your sinful heart to me and get on with the task of living life, depending on me."

Do you hear that? "Get on with the task of living life, depending on me." Don't be afraid of life. Live boldly and fully, trusting God with the outcome—he is truly *able* to bring beauty out of any ashes, to bring light out of any darkness. Take your eyes off of your sin and turn them onto your Father—let his love, power and grace transform you and equip you to forget sin and live passionately and fully for him. And when you fall—which you will—let him pick you up and allow him to redeem all of your failures, mess-ups and sins for good in your life. He *can do this* and he *will do this*—he has promised us that he will, as we choose to turn our life and struggles over to our Father.

Digging Deep

What's stirring in your heart now as you read these words? Is the Lord convicting you of a cautious life lived in fear of sinning? Is he showing you your buried talents? Ask him to show you all the ways in which your fear of his wrath and judgment—as well as the judgment of other Christians—has shackled you from living boldly for him. As he reveals your fears to you, confess this to your Father, and choose now to give that all up to him.

If you can, gather some pictures of yourself as a young child. See if you can find any where you're playing with abandon. What are you doing in those pictures? Do you remember what you dreamt of doing as a child? Back in the days when you could slay dragons, rescue damsels in distress or sail the ocean on quests around the world, what adventures did you imagine yourself pursuing?

Now think about all the things you've gravitated towards throughout your life. What talents did you show at an early age or have an aptitude for? Was it drawing? Writing? Dancing? Sports? Telling people about Jesus? Praying for your friends?

Now fast-forward throughout your life—teens, young adulthood, until now. Think about all of the dreams you didn't pursue. Think about the choices you've made along the way. Any regrets? Have you been living a "safe" life? No risks? Would people describe you as "nice" because you avoid conflict at all costs? Have you avoided speaking truth that needed to be said, words that needed to be shared about your Father?

This exercise is meant not to condemn you for your lost opportunities but to clear your account with your Father. Confess all of the choices you've made during the course of your life, both big and small, to bury your talents. Keep a short account with God as you write down all that your Father is showing you of how you've buried your talents. Remember to keep coming back to this list as you make decisions, both big and small, for your life moving forward. And ask him for the courage to "sin boldly," and watch what he does in your life.

CHAPTER 20

Let the Adventures Begin!

For I am about to do something new. See, I have already begun! Do you not see it? I will make a pathway through the wilderness. I will create rivers in the dry wasteland.

Isaiah 43:19, NLT

A number of years ago—completely without intending to—I ended up on a missions trip that took me to some of the most impoverished parts of South Africa. I say "without intending to" because I had always been one of those Christians who prayed (shuddering) that God would never call me to be a missionary or send me to a Third World country. To put this in context, think four-star resorts or cruises—that's me. My idea of a good vacation includes full-service coddling, lavish spa treatments, obsequious cabana boys and delectable gourmet food. And so I always assumed that I would never do anything crazy like travel somewhere where I'd have to use less-than-sanitary washroom facilities. What can I say? I have some OCD issues around cleanliness. Plus, seriously, how could I pack all of my shoes?

My adventures to Africa began rather innocuously. I really had no clue what the Lord had in store for me. Picture this: I was at a Christian counselling conference where Bruce Wilkinson of *The Prayer of Jabez* fame was speaking. Frankly, I was just there to get my continuing education credits, and it was at a luxurious hotel in California, so why not? Bruce began to speak out passionately about the people in Africa dying of AIDS and dealing with the horrific aftermath of violence, rape, death and loss. In a thundering voice (I think I heard the voice of God through Bruce at that moment), he shared that they desperately needed counsellors to come and help.

My heart started beating faster, and as he challenged us to stand up if we were willing to count ourselves "in," I found myself rising to my feet without any thought, almost as if I didn't have control over my limbs. My heart was beating so hard that I felt faint, but I was determined that I would stand up and risk it all for Jesus. I honestly think I heard angels singing, the moment was so intense.

And so I went, knowing very little about what to expect. I didn't know anyone else who was going, neither the organizers nor the participants. For those who know me well, this was very much out of character for me and a *huge* step outside of my comfort zone. I was anxious and fearful of what I would be facing in Africa, but I felt a certainty in my spirit that I was supposed to go, that I was preparing to go on an adventure that would stretch me and force me to rely on God. I had a sense that surrendering to God in this adventure would reap far more gain for me personally than I would ever be able to contribute to the suffering people in Africa.

For me, that was a pivotal turning point in my faith walk with God. It wasn't so much what I accomplished there, but it was learning to live in the Land of the Unknown, anticipating an adventure with my Father, trusting in his sovereignty and plans for my life. It was living in the "here and now"—the right-in-the-moment, minute-by-minute experience of walking closely with my Father, enjoying his presence and love, and seeing his handprint all over my life as well as the lives of many others. And oh, did I have the time of my life!

Even though I had initially signed up to do some counselling, God had other plans in mind for me. He knew that I needed to experience the African people personally, to break my heart and to put into my heart a passion and a compassion for the people. He wanted to give me a small window into the sorrow in his heart for the hurting people of Africa. I ended up working hands-on with the African people themselves, helping them plant gardens. This was part of Bruce Wilkinson's dream to overcome starvation in Africa, by enabling the people to be self-sufficient in feeding themselves. For those who know me, gardening is absolutely *not* my gift. But what a wonderful way to break from my comfort zone, to do something so tangible in helping the people.

An Ache in My Heart

During my time there, I fell in love with the country and the people. At the same time, it was incredibly heart-breaking to see all of the poverty and starvation and all the orphans. I spent much of my time there with my tears just in my chest, causing an ache in my heart. On many occasions, the tears spilled over, as I heard and saw the suffering experienced by so many. With sorrow, I learned that every 17 seconds a child in Africa dies from AIDS or starvation. I heard that there were over 15 million children living on the streets at that time, orphaned due to AIDS (the latest estimate, according to a 2012 survey, is 53.1 million).

With horror, I heard that many Africans believe that the only cure for AIDS is to have intercourse with a virgin, and hence babies were being raped by infected men. I also saw many teenage mothers living in very destitute conditions, hundreds of homes where the head of the household was six years old or younger, and households run by women, as the men had abandoned their families or died of AIDS.

At the same time, I experienced so much joy, as I had a chance to see the carefree happiness of the children and the sparkle in their eyes as their faces lit up with smiles when they were given beads and candy. Simple pleasures. I also saw the heartfelt faith of those who knew the Lord and the peace in their eyes as they trusted him to provide. Even the adults had the faith of a child, and because the Lord had shown himself faithful to them, they were filled with joy at his goodness. They had so little, yet their lives were filled with light and love and joy and peace. I felt God so strongly in their midst, and I could sense his very heartbeat for his people there.

I met many people in South Africa, many of whom stayed in my heart. One in particular was Maria, an 84–year-old grandmother who was the head of household of her family. She sat on a mat in front of her tin hut. I had the privilege of watching her sombre face light up with a smile when I put shiny beads around her neck and told her she was beautiful. When we asked her what she wanted, she asked for some cold water to drink, and I had the pleasure of giving her water and watching her face fill with gratitude for such a simple gift. These verses came to mind from Matthew 25:35–40: "*I was thirsty and you gave me something to drink…Truly I tell you, whatever you did for one of the least of these brothers and sisters of mine, you did for me.*"

I also had the privilege of visiting an AIDS clinic and hospice as a counsellor. I quickly realized that we had arrogance as North Americans, thinking we could come for a few days and somehow do any sort of counselling that would help the Africans. Not knowing anything about the language or the culture, we probably would have done more damage. But I had the opportunity to meet many South African volunteers, who loved the AIDS patients like they were their own families. Their mandate was to give these outcasts the best care they could, to show the love of Christ to these people. Jesus was very evident through their loving arms as they willingly hugged and held those AIDS patients and talked to them with such love and concern. My joy for that visit was to be able to be "Jesus with skin" as I too had a chance to show love to the patients, not by counselling them but by being a real person who just enjoyed being with them.

Missed Adventures

When I think back to my time in Africa, it still brings tears to my eyes. To think that I might have missed out on this life-changing experience if I had not stood up that day, heart pounding, having no clue what I was getting into but feeling a sense of urgency to follow God. How many adventures have I missed out on because I refused to surrender to God and trust in his plan for my life? I haven't always remembered that moment in my decisions of late and in the day-to-day way I live my life. Sometimes still—all too often—I take the "safe" route and go with what I know rather than venture into the Land of the Unknown.

But this I know with complete certitude: my desire to be live life fully, to walk closely with my Father, to know that I am doing what he created me to do as a beloved daughter is only possible with my decision to surrender to him in the adventure of life, and to trust him in *all* things. To live life boldly. To take risks. To love others extravagantly, even foolishly. To walk in the Land of the Unknown with an attitude of positive anticipation for what God is doing in the adventure of my life.

John Eldredge says it well in his book *Waking the Dead:*

If you're not pursuing a dangerous quest with your life, well, then, you don't need a Guide. If you haven't found yourself in the midst of a ferocious war, then you won't need a seasoned Captain. If you've settled in your mind to live as though this is a fairly neutral world and you are simply trying to live your life as best you can, then you can probably get by with the Christianity of tips and techniques. Maybe. I'll give you about a fifty-fifty chance. But if you intend to live in the Story that God is telling, and if you want the life he offers, then you are going to need more than a handful of principles, however noble they may be. There are too many twists and turns in the road ahead, too many ambushes waiting only God knows where, too much at stake. You cannot possibly prepare yourself for every situation. Narrow is the way, said Jesus. How shall we be sure to find it? We need God intimately, and we need him desperately.[60]

A Journey with Jesus

Just recently, during my time of winter, I was feeling frantic to hear from God, for him to bring salve to my battered heart and to give me a sense of hope to help me through the deadness of this season. I knew that I was at a crossroads in my life, that as he was leading me to let go and allow the old things to die in the winter, he was also leading me into an unknown future where much fruit was going to spring forth. And in his wonderful grace, my Father gave me a beautiful picture of me on a white water raft with Jesus.

Over the months of winter, God gave me a series of images, all in this theme. Initially, I was alone on my raft in the stormy waters, battered about against the sharp rocks, so fearful and using all my strength to stay afloat. I fought off the waters with my oar, exhausted and desperate. Just when I was about to give up and capsize, Jesus came on board. He gently took the oar from my hands and commanded me to rest. And then he took over, managing the churning waters with ease. Even as he did, the waters did not calm. Though he had the power, I sensed he wanted me to experience surrender and trust, to rest in him even when danger was all around me. When I could see the supreme confidence and peace on his face as he navigated my raft for me, I grew in confidence.

And then, after a time of rest, I saw Jesus hand me my own oar (much smaller than his) and instruct me to follow his lead, mimicking his moves right behind him. I didn't know where we were going, but I didn't have to navigate. I just had to follow and trust him. And as I saw this picture, I heard the Lord saying,

"Enjoy the ride! Look around and see the beauty all around you, let yourself experience the excitement of our adventure together! Breathe in all this splendour around you. I will give you the gift of abundant joy through all of this if you keep your eyes on me and trust that you are safe in my hands. Though there's so much uncertainty, turmoil and danger for you, we are moving forward. I have a plan for your life and I am directing your raft through it. And remember we're moving forward, even when you feel stuck."

God Rigs Our World

Do you believe God has rigged the world so that fullest life only works when we embrace risk and live by faith? This is good news, because all our own attempts to find a safer life, to live by the expectations of others, kill our souls.

Safe is not how we were meant to live.

Pete Wilson says in his book *Plan B,* "We've got to take that risk if we're going to live the kind of lives God has called us to live, to be the people dreamed of when he thought us into existence."[61] When Jesus said to take up our cross and follow him, he knew that it meant terrible risk and possible loss, even death hanging upside down on a cross, as Peter ended up experiencing by his own choice. *"For the joy set before him [Jesus] endured the cross"* (Hebrews 12:2).

A few days later, during my quiet time with God, he spoke to me yet again about riding on the raft with him:

"Remember the picture I gave you of riding the raft in rough waters? Yes, there are risks but the number one experience you will have is excitement and enjoyment, plus a deep sense of your safety and future in my hands. Last time we talked about it, you were focused on the rocks and risks and bumpy parts of the ride. This time, I want you to picture us having the time of our lives—we're laughing as the spray gets us wet. What a rush! It's gorgeous on this river. See the beautiful forests we pass, hear the sounds of the birds and smell the water and nature. See the bright sun shining. Most of all, hear us laughing, 'Here comes a big one! Wooooooo!' I'm standing up, trying to rock the boat, and I'm reaching over the raft to splash you with water. Oh, we're having the time of our lives! And that's just the beginning. Remember even as we are enjoying the experience of the journey, we're also headed somewhere. We are moving forward. My daughter, I love hanging out with you. It's never a duty but always a joy and a delight!"

How often do we lose sight of this? As we traverse through all the toils and dangers of adventuring with God, there is so much to bring us joy and delight as we choose to pay attention and notice. I know I struggled to understand the extravagance of God and instead pictured a life of following him to mean only sacrifice, suffering, and deprivation. Don't get me wrong—there are no guarantees that we will avoid suffering. God has warned us we will have trouble (John 16:33). But if I choose instead to focus on the experience of the ride, notice the beauty around me and the simple pleasures he is showing me, if I delight in a life that's lived in full communion with my Father, then perhaps I will be living a life that is exactly as he's created me to live.

And as I envisioned my journey with Jesus on the raft, I heard the convicting words of my Father:

"The hope growing in your heart is such a tentative thing. You do not believe that I can be so extravagant and give you your dreams (and far beyond) just because. Look at creation around you—do you not see my extravagance? The abundance of beauty is for you and is of no practical purpose other than to delight—delight you and delight me as it draws you to me. I love to give great, extravagant gifts merely to savour. Why do you see me as such a stingy Father? Think about how you love to delight by giving your kids gifts they want and how it gladdens your heart to see their joy. How much more am I able to do that and want to do that for you! I love delighting my beloved children! Can you not trust that I can do anything? I can continue to stretch you and grow you even while I give you extravagant gifts. Ask and you shall receive, knock and the door will open, seek and you shall find. Ask me. I have a knack for doing exceedingly, abundantly more than you ask or imagine!"

The Dangerous and Unpredictable Flow

I don't know about you, but I'm ready for a life of adventure with our Father. I refuse to return to my life of drudgery and safety. I choose instead to live a life of journeying on the wild, unpredictable and dangerous rapids of a life lived fully for God. Even as I choose this life, I am realizing that maybe this river I'm in, this risky, dangerous, powerful, unpredictable raging, isn't the dangers of life but a representation of God's Spirit—powerful, dangerous, beautiful, implacable, forceful—yet breathtakingly beautiful. Being in the flow of his Spirit is scary and unpredictable yet deeply adventurous and fulfilling, the way life is meant to be lived. Don't fight it; go with it. Being in the flow is the point. Being in the flow *is* the adventure, and along the way, there will be many experiences and encounters.

Lest you think that a life of adventure isn't for you, that somehow God only has big plans for "important" people, consider the ordinary, common people God has chosen throughout the history of humanity. He picked an unknown teenage girl to bring his Son into the world; He chose a simple fisherman to be the "rock" upon which his Church was built; he chose a young Jewish girl called Anne Frank to teach us about the suffering of his people during the Nazi occupation; he picked a dairy farmer's son, Billy Graham, to bring the gospel to millions of people worldwide. God doesn't choose only those who are smarter, more gifted or more eloquent than you are. God chooses us regular folks.

But there is a catch: God looks for people who are willing to live on the edge—people who have a deep longing for a life of significant impact. People who believe that he can and will do the impossible through them. People who are willing to be foolish for God, who are *desperate* to see God move profoundly in this fallen, broken world of ours, who long to see their dreams come to fruition—dreams to change the world.

Joy Is Our Birthright

I don't know about you, but I want to be one of those people who so long to see God's agenda fulfilled in this world that they attempt what seems impossible. What about you? Don't miss out on all that your Father has intended for you. Don't let *anything* steal away your joy in an adventure with your Father. Mark Buchanan in *Spiritual Rhythms* reminds us, "Joy is our birthright. Joy is a sign of the Messiah's presence, the wine at his banqueting table. Joy is the savor and aroma of heaven itself."[62] Don't let your fears or wrong theology steal away from you that which is your birthright:

> For some reason, most of us, even those of us (like me) with pagan roots, carry a residue of Protestant angst that makes us feel guilty if we feel good. This is odd, given that we follow a Savior who is borderline obsessed that his joy fill us to overflowing. Odd, given we worship a King who's first miracle…was to turn water into wine, for no greater reason that that the party might go on. Odd, given that we take our ethical cues largely from the apostle who wrote, "Finally, my brothers and sisters, rejoice in the Lord!…Rejoice in the Lord always. I will say it again: Rejoice!"[63]

In case you get the wrong idea that a life of adventure for you necessarily means a life in the spotlight doing Billy-Graham-type evangelism or Mother-Teresa-like ministry, let me state emphatically that this is not about becoming famous or visible or changing the entire world at large. A life of adventure for *you* means a life lived fully as your Father has created you to be and the life situation he has placed you in—whether as a stay-at-home mother or retired businessperson or waste collector. Some of the greatest men and women God has used to change this world will never be known by most of us this side of heaven, as they've toiled behind the scenes.

But for those of you who *are* wired to pursue public ministry, don't let false humility or fear of being viewed as prideful or ambitious by others prevent you from doing what God has called you to do. Sometimes he *does* call us to positions in this world that are very public and visible and lead to fame. I know, for myself, a lot of what has held me back is a secret shame that I carry in my heart a longing to have a massive impact on this world through my words, either in writing or in the spotlight speaking.

Instead of embracing how God has wired me, I kept my dreams hidden and under tight control, chastising myself for my pride and self-seeking ambition. It is only as I have come to listen to my voice and to trust my Father's heart that I have come to see the schemes of the enemy devilishly pitting my desire to honour God against me, by convincing me that my dreams were rooted in pride and could not be from God. Twisting his vision for me to speak was his sneaky way of shutting down what God wanted to do in and through my life—and he was almost successful as I ended up in burnout, living a life I wasn't meant to pursue.

As I mentioned earlier, a life of adventure is about discovering the buried treasures that our Father has implanted into each of our hearts from the beginning of time. But beyond discovering the treasures, the adventure is in pursuing them full out, expecting more than anything you can do in your own strength or imagination. *It's not about what other people think.* But it's about trusting in God and relying on his strength and power to do whatever he chooses in and through you *exceedingly, abundantly beyond* what you can even begin to imagine.

Don't Quit!

A few years ago, I quit a call in my life. That's been one of my biggest regrets. After coming home from Africa, I was on fire for God, ready to take on the world. Determined to do my part to get the word out, I wrote letters, posted pictures and even got up on the podium to speak of my experiences in Africa. With tears pouring down my face (and those were ugly tears, the kind where you're snorting so hard you can barely speak), I laid my heart out before our congregation, certain that they would be as moved as I was. *Nothing.* I asked for people to commit to help. Still nothing.

I followed up by email to a contact I'd made in Africa. This was a pastor running the AIDS hospice I visited, and we had chatted about my returning to train the locals how to counsel those who were sick. I knew that I was supposed to do this! Email after email—no response. So what did I do? I gave up. I got busy with the stuff of life again.

Several years later, I sat in the office of our executive pastor as he shared his passion for the African people. Yes! He would love for me to come and train the locals in caring for the raped, abused and broken people of Africa! My heart pounded with excitement at the thought of getting back. But then I went home and hit a wall of resistance from my family—there was too much going on for me to leave. So what did I do? Again, I gave up.

Today, I struggle to break free from the apathy in my spirit. It has been a bondage that has prevented me from living out the adventure of my life. But even now, as I examine the longing in my soul for a dangerous quest, I can hear God's call once again. I've been praying for the last few months about my heart for the abused and abandoned children in this world. My heart hurts especially for those who have been abducted and forced into the sex trafficking industry. *God, can I get involved somehow?*

And then, just this past weekend, I met a pastor who is involved in the rescue of children from sex trafficking and is establishing safe houses in Cambodia and Vietnam. A coincidence? Of the hundred women at the conference I was at, why did God choose me to sit with her? Was it a divine appointment?

I don't know what the future holds, but I am determined to grab hold of the adventures God has for me. I want to live to the full. For I know that to do anything less is a life of bondage—a "safe" life, yes, but a life sucked dry of the joy and passion that is our birthright.

Yes, a life of adventure with God is also a life where there are many dangers and much toil. *It can be hard work.* We think that just because we're on an adventure with God, it should be all fun and games, and we forget that pursuing a life with God can be dangerous. And so the temptation is strong to quit midway, to get off of the raft, to exit early. It just gets too tough. The work, the sweat, the hassle, the heartbreak—it doesn't seem worth it. Egypt looks good when the desert gets too hot.

Don't give up. Don't quit halfway through your adventure. Remember that your adventure starts and ends with your Father, that he *is* the adventure. This isn't about running off to Africa at the drop of a hat or selling everything to give to the poor (although he may call you to such adventures)—it is about living in God, allowing him to live through you, and choosing to experience joy and adventure in your journey with him.

Digging Deep

If a life of adventure with God is unfathomable to you, ask God to show you what is preventing you from living a life full out for him. Have you given up on God? Are you filled with doubts, fears and questions that are preventing you from trusting him? Or is your life so busy that you don't have time to listen to his call to embark on an adventure with you? What are the deep disappointments or hard knocks or tedious stretches that you might have to endure this side of beginning your adventure with God? What dangers and toils are you currently experiencing that may be tempting you to quit midway? What does a life of adventure with God look like for you?

Take the time now to prepare yourself for your adventure. Consider what is blocking you and then consider what the Lord is asking you to do.

Ready to begin your adventure?

Pull out your journal or computer, take a deep breath and begin with this prayer:

Lord, I confess that I have been living a "safe" life. I haven't been living the life of adventure you call me to. Please help me understand what has held me back. [Write down whatever thoughts that the Lord brings to your mind—whether it's fear, unbelief, wanting to stay in control of your own life, difficulty trusting God, discouragement because the obstacles have seemed insurmountable, allowing the naysayers in your life influence your decisions. Keep writing everything that comes to mind.] *Please forgive me, Lord, for* _____ [list everything that has come to mind]. I choose now to trust and embrace the life you've called me to. Help me to hear you and my heart about the adventures I long to pursue but have always doubted could ever happen.

Now here is where you need to abandon all doubts that hold you back and take the time to listen to your heart. If you were to list three things that you would love to do—if money were no object and there were no practical issues to consider—what would they be? (You can choose to say win a lottery, but I want you to dig deeper and consider your *dreams,* not just having lots of money or material wealth.) If you could be anything you wanted to be, what would that be?

If this is hard for you to do, take your time, and don't give up. Some of us have never been taught to dream, and so it's hard for us to even know our own heart and passions. Just keep praying for God to show you your heart and the adventures he has in store for you. Keep coming back to this exercise until you can answer these questions. Talk to friends and family who know you well. If you have a genuine openness to adventure in your life, the Lord will lead you.

If you know the three things you'd love to do, I want you to commit them to the Keeper of your dreams now. Pray from your heart, allowing your longing to speak honestly to God. Again, I would encourage you to pray continuously for these things.

Lest you think these dreams are for the very distant future, I want you to ask your Father to begin to lay out the path for you to pursue your adventures. Ask him, "What are you asking me to give up?" (Write down everything that comes to mind.) "What are you asking me to risk right *now?*" (Write down all that the Lord shows you.)

Commit *now* to obeying the Lord and giving up what he's asking you and risking what he's calling you to do. Share the results of this exercise with a trusted friend. Dare to speak it out loud so that it becomes even more real to you. And strap on your seat belt!

CHAPTER 21

Fullest Freedom

But whoever did want him, who believed he was who he claimed and would do what he said, He made to be their true selves, their child-of-God selves.

John 1:12, MSG

I stared in amazement at Clarissa with my jaw dropped. After a brief moment of shock, I quickly rushed over to give her a hug. I had not seen her for five years until today at a conference where I was speaking. I could not believe how she'd changed! Peace radiated from her, and this incredible beauty glowed from within. When I heard she was going to be one of the speakers, I was stunned, but I also sensed I was walking on sacred ground. And now I was witnessing a life transformed by our good Father.

Shivers tickled down my spine to hold this great Masterwork of a restored life!

When I'd met Clarissa five years before, she was timid and fearful, hardly able to speak her name, let alone get up on a stage to speak. She had been suffering from severe anxiety and agoraphobia, so traumatized from some wounding experiences and losses that she had almost completely shut down from life. In fact, she had come very close to cancelling her plans to attend the conference. But with the encouragement of some friends and a deep sense she was meant to be there, with fear and trembling she'd stepped into the wild river of God's Holy Spirit. That was the day her adventure began.

Looking back, I could see God's hand all over it—in my life and in hers. I remembered he'd given me this burning message to share that I crafted into a presentation I called Surrendered Faith—from which parts of this book were formed—all before I was even asked to speak. When the invitation came, I knew in my spirit that I was to share this message, with no idea of the impact it would have on lives, and one in particular. As I shared passionately about what a life of living free of fear was like and how choosing to live in surrendered faith was transformational, Clarissa was listening intently, hearing each word as if directed solely to her.

I hadn't noticed her until the end of the weekend, when I invited the women to stand and share what had especially impacted them. She told me later she was almost fainting with nerves, but she couldn't resist the pull of her Father. With tears streaming down her face, Clarissa had shared her journey, as the women cried to hear how the Lord had led her to this conference. She committed right there to living a life of surrender. And when I led the women in prayer, Clarissa had been the most fervent supplicant, kneeling with her hands raised high, determinedly mouthing the words after me. She laid down her fears in each aspect of her life, one by one.

Fast-forward five years, and I was looking at a different woman—one who was *free*. Free to live life with joy and peace; free from the fears that held her back; free to live in the flow of the Holy Spirit and be all God created her to be. As she shared with me all God was doing in and through her, I could only marvel. She was now working with children in a ministry that required daily interaction with people—something she used to freeze up about—and she absolutely loved it. Her relationships were thriving as she discovered more of her voice and set healthy boundaries, expressed her opinions and opened her heart to more and more people. What an extraordinary testimony she was to me!

And oh, what an amazing Father we have!

You Can Be Who You *Really* Are

Brennan Manning says it beautifully when he reminds us,

One of the wonderful results of my consciousness of God's staggering love for me as I am is a freedom not to be who I should be or who others want me to be. I can be who I really am...It is the real me that God loves. I don't have to be anyone else...God says, "I love you so you'll change." I simply expose myself to the love that is everything and have an immense, unshakeable, reckless, raging confidence that God loves me so much he'll change me and fashion me into the child that he always wanted me to be.[64]

Do you hear that? A freedom to be *who you really are*. A freedom from the painful shackles of your crippling fears, your self-rejecting shame, your deep-rooted and hidden insecurities, your desperate search for worth, and fear of God's expectations.

And who are you? Contrary to pop psychology and what we're often taught by the world, "The answer to the question," Manning says, "'Who am I?' comes not from self-analysis but through personal commitment. The heart converted from mistrust to *trust in the irreversible forgiveness of Jesus Christ* is nothing less than a new creation, and all ambiguity about personal identity is blown away."[65]

But in striving to be the *me* I want to be, I have to ask myself, "What is it I really want?" I want to be fully alive inside. I want the inner freedom to live in love and joy. I want to be the woman God created me to be. I want to be the best version of me. I've had glimpses of the *me* I was created to be. When I really connect with clients and see the light go on in their faces when I encourage them. When I give some food to a homeless person. When I hug my son rather than yell at him when he's feeling anxious. When I stand up and speak truth into a difficult situation.

This is the *me* I want to be.

The Best Version of You

As I do all these things, I catch a glimpse of why God made me. Only God knows my full potential, and he is guiding me toward the best version of myself all the time. He is never in a hurry, and he never gets discouraged by how long it takes or how many times I mess up. He's delighted every time I grow. For I am—we *all* are—God's handiwork. We are *his* creation. Our whole lives are his canvas on which he creates.

When I realize he has created good things for me to do as signposts to the real me, I am overjoyed. God made me to flourish as I become even more of my true self. And as God helps me grow, I will change, but I will still be me. Just a *better* me. He prewired my temperament. He determined my natural gifts and abilities. I don't need to become anyone else or wear masks to gain acceptance. He wants to *redeem* everyone, not exchange us for someone else. I will never become the analytical and logical thinker that my husband is—no matter how much I wish I were like him when I'm feeling too emotional. I will never be the dynamic and hilarious entertainer my friend is, no matter how hard I try. That's not who I was created to be.

How can I be fully me? Brennan Manning points out the way:

> Only in a relationship of the deepest intimacy can we allow another person to know us as we truly are. It is difficult enough for us to live with the awareness of our stinginess and shallowness, our anxieties and infidelities, but to disclose our dark secrets to another is intolerably risky.[66]

Only when I can be fully confident that I'll be loved and accepted by my Father in all of my sinful and broken ways can I begin to discover all he's created in me.

But the journey starts in the soul empowered by God's Spirit. *Flourishing* means being connected to God's Spirit, allowing him to control your thoughts and actions. It's the choice to fully surrender to the resurrecting life of Jesus Christ that allows his love to redeem your story as you venture out and risk and trust. When my spirit is flourishing, I am most fully alive. I have a purpose for living. I am drawn to put on virtue and put off sin. I am most fully *me.*

The entirety of my life begins to be transformed. When I am flourishing, my mind is marked by joy and peace. I am curious and love to learn. Along with my spirit and mind, when I am flourishing, my time begins to be transformed as well. When I wake up it's with a feeling of expectancy. I begin to receive each moment as a gift from God. My flourishing self pours into my relationships. I enjoy people, I listen and I care. I am open and vulnerable and invite intimacy. I quickly admit my errors and freely forgive.

So how do I assess myself these days? In John Ortberg's book *The Me I Want to Be,* he challenges us to ask ourselves two questions: Am I growing more easily discouraged these days? Am I growing more easily irritated these days?[67] Do I struggle with discouragement and irritation? Am I *tired* of faking it and trying to live the Christian life in my own strength? Am I beginning to learn that the core of a flourishing soul is the love of God and the peace of God? If peace is growing in me, I am not easily discouraged. If love is growing, I am not easily irritated.

Get that? It's God in me. My Father in me and through me.

Death to the Fake Me

But we don't just drift into being the best versions of ourselves. If I want to be the real me, I have to be aware of all the times I try to fake it. Pretending to be someone we're not is hard work—take it from me, a recovered faker. That's why we often feel so drained after a situation where we feel like we have to be "on," such as public speaking or a first date where we feel like we have to project a certain image rather than just be ourselves. I don't know about you, but I'm drawn to transparency and long to be where I can just be myself. It's a relief not to have to pretend to pray more than we really do or know our Bible inside and out—especially when we fear being one step away from being discovered as a fraud. We never have to pretend with God; genuine brokenness pleases him more than pretend spirituality.

I also have to be aware of the me I think I *should* be. When my kids were younger, I used to feel guilty and less spiritual for not getting up an hour early each day to read my Bible, never thinking that the love and care I gave my kids counted as "spiritual" activity. It never occurred to me that I was serving God more faithfully than someone else who reads her Bible daily but neglects her kids or treats them with anger and impatience. I used to struggle with feeling like a failure as a Christian because I wasn't diligent in praying consistently for others. My mom is an incredible prayer warrior, and she will spend hours a day praying through lists of people. But me, I'd be lucky if I shot off a quick prayer for a friend if I happened to think of her. I didn't realize that the way I was loving people counted and delighted God because he wired me to be deeply relational.

Henri Nouwen wrote, "Spiritual greatness has nothing to do with being greater than others. It has everything to do with being as great as each of us can be."[68] Like many people, I grew up believing I needed to be more driven and energetic than I really am. I saw myself as a go-getter who liked charging ahead to conquer the next mountain. But just today, I experienced burnout again, trying to be this false me. Pride and my need for approval and acceptance got the better of me. To let that image of myself go requires a continual death because I was tied into that me for so long. Only through God's love am I learning to accept the true me, the one who can say no, be tired and allow myself more rest and downtime.

I realized too that when I was growing up, my mom placed many of her dreams on me. She had wanted to be a doctor, but because of life circumstances, she was never able to achieve that goal. She constantly told me I was a lot like her when I was growing up, and so I ended up taking on a lot of her persona. I would get completely nauseated at the sight of blood, so I decided instead at a very early age to become a psychologist—a head doctor. While I don't regret my decision, the choices I have made have brought scars, a loss of me at many points in my life, and a wearing of a multitude of masks to fulfill what others wanted me to be. I've wandered away from the adventures the Lord meant for me because of trying to be the "me" I thought I should be—the "me" that others told me I was or validated me for being.

We Are Not Factory Produced

When we allow God's Spirit to direct our transformation, we *accept* that we are completely unique. I accept that the way I become the best version of myself isn't following a prescribed way but listening to the Spirit of God in me. Listening to my heart.

The Fully Lived Life

God *never* grows two people the same way. The Bible contains countless individual journeys—no two are the same. God is a handcrafter. He doesn't do one-size-fits-all. Disciples are not factory produced. We are *free*. No wonder we get frustrated when we think we're supposed to look like the pastor or someone we're currently learning from. We all learn differently, struggle differently and relate to God differently.

The Spirit of God flows best when we come as we are, in transparency. When I am in relationships where I can be real with my struggles, where I am accepted fully even in my brokenness, then I am in relationships that are life-giving. And through that, the Spirit of God flows.

Stand Up and Be Counted

So where are you with this quest for the real you? Are you living the life you were meant to live? Or are you recognizing in the arid dryness of your soul the possibility that you were meant to live a life of fullness and freedom to be you as God intended you to be?

Do you know your personality? Your passions? Your likes and dislikes? Your values? What makes you, *you?*

If you don't know the answers to these questions, choose to find out! Ask your closest friends and family who know you well—ask them what your strengths and weaknesses are. Or go see a psychologist who specializes in assessments and do some questionnaires that will help you pinpoint who you are. Or go see a life coach who can help you walk through this journey of self-discovery.

But be aware: everyone has an agenda for you. Powerful others will try to make you conform and live up to their expectations. You will have to face being defiant and going against them. *Your life will depend on this.* Parents, spouses, children, pastors, friends and co-workers—the people around you—will want you to be the you they think you should be.

If I spend my life trying to be *that* me, I will never be free. Loving people means disappointing them sometimes. Jesus loved everyone but he disappointed and angered people at times.

To love someone is to desire and work towards the best version of them. The only one who can do that for *you* is God.

Failure to Thrive

One of the biggest mental health issues I see on a regular basis isn't depression or anxiety; it's a failure to thrive, to flourish—someone who is languishing. *Languishing* is when someone is able to function but has lost a sense of hope and meaning. It's not the presence of mental illness; it's the absence of mental and emotional vitality. If that is you, wait no longer! Choose to break free. Choose life as God intended you to live.

Don't wait for circumstances to change for your life to begin. Freedom and joy are possible *now*. When your primary focus is being present with God, everything else has a way of falling into place. Jesus made staggering promises about how he can transform lives. He said, "*Let anyone who is thirsty come to me and drink. Whoever believes in me...rivers of living water will flow from within them*" (John 7:37–39).

The Holy Spirit is always ready to guide you into the best version of yourself. God knows it will take time to develop the habits of staying in the flow of the Spirit, and he is ever-patient and tenacious. He asks only that our hearts remain sincere and open, not that we try hard not to screw up. God looks at the heart.

Come to Your Father as a Child

Why is "Christian living" so often about the shoulds? We are so afraid of others' judgment and God's disapproval that we trap ourselves into being a "good Christian." Who said we should trudge through life-fulfilling responsibilities? Scripture tells us to come to God as a child. Their simple faith and dependency, and also their simple enjoyment of life, is a life of freedom. I think back to my son when he was two, shrieking away at each present he opened—his total delight with the good gifts he received. When did we lose that? We became so down-trodden, so burdened, we don't even notice all the great gifts God gives on a daily basis.

There will always be heartaches. But focus on the joys, the gifts, the laughter and the fun of life, and rest in your Father's capable hands with complete trust. Not ignoring the realities of life but focusing instead on the bigger reality of God in full control, sovereign over all things. Nothing happens without his permission. Nothing takes him by surprise. If he allows something bad to happen, can he redeem it for good? Focusing on the "realities" won't actually change them. Like a child, trust your parent to teach and guide you and protect you from all long-term harm. And get on with the business of living with joy!

Over my season of winter, how consistently he expressed his love and grace. I could not have invented such love. No matter how I whined or complained, no matter how discouraged or misdirected I got, my Father was always there. His compassion and love were always foremost. Contrary to the way I used to see God, my soul now breathes with relief; the shackles of guilt and self-criticism are always falling away.

Living Out of Our Father's Grace

Towards the end of my journey out of darkness I journalled,

Papa, I want to love and live extravagantly, to live out of grace and not fear. I've heard pastors who are strong on truth but weak on grace say we have to be careful we don't take advantage of your grace to do whatever we want. But there's something not quite right with this. I think if I can truly accept your love and grace, if I can be resting in your love—my heart then longs only to love you and follow you. I long to live my life fully for you. Ultimately, my only chance of living the holy life comes from your Spirit in me—who operates best in a heart softened by much love and grace—not one rooted in fear or duty.

Papa, you know the mistakes I will make in learning to live life authentically as me, but that is part of the process. I need not fear mistakes—all of that was dealt with at the cross. I refuse to live life in the sidelines. I have to learn through living life—not always fretting about making the "perfect" decision. I have no need to fear sin and my sinful nature—because you love me. Let me receive your love with my sinful, imperfect heart that needs you desperately.

You see us as holy and blameless because of Jesus' redemptive work on the cross. "It is finished." Why do we have such a hard time grasping this? Why would we need shame and penance for our sins when it's been finished?! Thank you, Papa. Thank you! Thank you! I can never stop thanking you for this gift to me.

You've given me new life so that now, new life is me. I am ready to burst forth from the land that has been lying fallow, after a winter of death. I am the life being born. Thank you, Papa! Thank you! You are the new life in me!

And so our journey together comes to an end.

I pray that you may grasp how immeasurably high and wide and deep is your Father's love for you, a child of the Most High King. You are able to *break free* from whatever and whoever has held you back. And if you accept the invitation to a life of *fullness* with your Father, you will begin the adventure he has planned for you. It's his promise to you.

Listen to what your Father has to say to you (adapted from Ephesians 1:3–19, MSG):

> Long before I laid down earth's foundations, I had *you* in mind, had settled on you as the focus of my love, to be made *whole* and *holy* by my love. Long, long ago I decided to adopt you into *my* family through Jesus Christ. (What *pleasure* I took in planning this!) I wanted you to enter into the celebration of my *lavish* gift-giving by the hand of my beloved Son. Because of the sacrifice of the Messiah, you're a *free* people—free of penalties and punishments chalked up by all your misdeeds. And not just barely free, either. *Abundantly free!* It's in Christ that you find out *who you are* and what you are living for. Long before you first heard of Christ and got your hopes up, I had my eye on you, had designs on you for *glorious living!*

So as I end, my prayer for you is that "with both feet planted firmly on love, you'll be able to take in with all followers of Jesus the *extravagant* dimensions of Christ's love. Reach out and experience the breadth! Test its length! Plumb the depths! Rise to the heights! *Live full lives, full in the fullness of God.*"

May you always live the fully lived life of freedom and joy that is your promise in Jesus!

Acknowledgements

Little did I know all that was involved in writing and publishing a book! If it weren't for God's generosity in providing remarkable people to guide me, I know I'd still be bumbling my way through this!

I am so grateful for the encouragement, wisdom and perspective brought by the gifted Mick Silva, editor extraordinaire (and a pretty darn amazing writer himself). I am also humbled by Sheri Silva's heart to serve, and her input to this book has been invaluable. You are some seriously great folks! Thank you for your love for God and for teaching me how to share his love through story. And thank you for pushing me (!) to let down my walls and be transparent so I could reflect God's incredible grace and love. You both have been such a gift to me.

While my path to publishing has been anything but straightforward, I am so thankful the Lord led me to Larry and Marina Willard of Castle Quay Publishing. Your knowledge of the publishing world has been invaluable, and I thank you for going above and beyond with your wonderful care and guidance. I so appreciate your personal involvement in the myriad of details involved in launching a book. You guys rock!

I am moved to tears by the support of my wonderful friends (in no particular order): Elizabeth, Terri-Lynn, Scott, Lorie, Pamela, Gillian, Wendy, Linda, Pam, Doug, Cathy and Leanne. I honestly couldn't have done it without your love and prayers. I know you have stood in the gap for me, especially during the difficult parts of this journey. I am still blown away by how God perfectly times those words of encouragement and prayers from you! I also want to especially mention my dear sister-in-law, Susan, for believing in me, praying for me and being such a steadfast friend to me. You are amazing.

To my mentor, Adrienne: I am forever grateful for the years you have invested in me. You have been grace personified to me. There is no one who reflects Jesus better to me than you.

To my mom, Lily: Words can't express my gratitude for your years of love and prayer and for your timely words of wisdom. I know you have always been in my corner. Thank you for your unshakeable belief in me.

More than 30 years ago, the Lord brought my safe place to me through my husband, Peter. You have been my rock and strength. God has used you to bring much healing to my life. Thank you for your steadfast love that has anchored me through the ups and downs of life. Your unwavering support has been life-giving to me.

I am so grateful for the gift of my kids, Amanda and Cameron. When I first prayed for you years ago, I could not have imagined how wonderfully God would answer my prayers! Amanda, you are much loved and gifted with an immense capacity to love others generously. Your courage to stand strong for your faith blows me away. Cam, you are my B2. I am so proud of how you're growing up to be a young man of integrity, perseverance and kindness.

And Papa? You are my everything.

About Dr. Merry C. Lin

Dr. Lin is a licensed psychologist and clinical director of LifeCare Centres (www.lifecarecentres.com), with over 20 years of clinical experience. She is valued by clients and professionals as a compassionate counsellor and trusted speaker.

Dr. Lin is married, with two children, and she is a member of a local church in Ontario, Canada, where she is involved in several care ministries. When relaxing, she can be found curled up with a good book or spending time with her family.

Visit her website www.drmerrylin.com to learn more about her or to subscribe to her blog "Ask Dr. Merry." You can also follow her on Facebook, www.facebook.com/drmerrylin.

Endnotes

[1] Brent Curtis and John Eldredge, *The Sacred Romance: Drawing Closer to the Heart of God* (Nashville: Thomas Nelson, 1997), 49–50.

[2] John Piper, *A Godward Life: Savoring the Supremacy of God in All of Life* (Sisters: Multnomah Publishers, Inc., 1997), 173.

[3] Oswald Chambers, *My Utmost for his Highest, Updated Edition in Today's Language* (Grand Rapids: Discovery House Publishers, 1992), August 29th devotional.

[4] William P. Young, *The Shack* (Newbury Park: Windblown Media, 2007), 179.

[5] Young, *The Shack,* 180.

[6] Young, *The Shack,* 197–198.

[7] Young, *The Shack,* 205–206.

[8] Dallas Willard, *The Divine Conspiracy: Rediscovering Our Hidden Life in God* (New York: Harper Collins, 1997), 41.

[9] John Ortberg, *The Me I Want to Be: Becoming God's Best Version of You* (Grand Rapids: Zondervan, 2010), 59.

[10] Simon Tugwell, *The Beatitudes: Soundings in Christian Traditions* (Springfield: Templegate Publishers, 1980), 130.

[11] Thomas Merton, *Thoughts in Solitude* (New York: Farrar, Straus and Giroux, 1999 edition), 34.

[12] Curtis and Eldredge, *The Sacred Romance,* 5.

[13] Brennan Manning and Jim Hancock, *Posers, Fakers and Wannabes* (Colorado Springs: NavPress, 2007), 37–38.

[14] Manning and Hancock, *Posers, Fakers and Wannabes,* 38–39.

[15] Manning and Hancock, *Posers, Fakers and Wannabes,* 48.

[16] Manning and Hancock, *Posers, Fakers and Wannabes,* 51.

[17] Carl G. Jung, *Modern Man in Search of a Soul* (New York: Harcourt, Brace and World Harvest Books, 1933), 235.

[18] Brennan Manning, *Abba's Child: The Cry of the Heart for Intimate Belonging* (Colorado Springs: NavPress, 2002), 22–23.

[19] Anthony DeMello, *The Way to Love: Meditations for Life* (New York: Doubleday, 1992), 63–64.

[20] John Eldredge, *Walking with God: Talk to Him. Hear from Him. Really* (Nashville: Thomas Nelson 2008), 87.

[21] Os Hillman, *Today God is First* (Elkton: Church Growth Institute, 2012), online devotional *Prime Time with God,* posted online February 10, 2012.

[22] Mark Buchanan, *Spiritual Rhythms: Being with Jesus Every Season of Your Soul* (Grand Rapids: Zondervan, 2010), 34–36.

[23] Hillman, *Prime Time with God,* devotional posted online, March 27, 2012.

[24] Dan Allender, *To Be Told: Know Your Story, Shape Your Future* (Colorado Springs: Waterbrook Press, 2005), chapter 3, e-book edition.

[25] Henri J. M. Nouwen, *The Inner Voice of Love: A Journey Through Anguish to Freedom* (New York: Image Books, Doubleday, 1998), 47–48.

[26] Nouwen, *The Inner Voice of Love,* 26–27.

[27] Julian of Norwich, *The Revelations of Divine Love* (New York: Cosimo, 2007 edition, originally published in 1927), 148.

[28] Milan and Kay Yerkovich, *How We Love: Discover Your Love Style, Enhance Your Marriage* (Colorado Springs: WaterBrook Press, 2008).

[29] Manning and Hancock, *Posers, Fakers and Wannabes,* 24.

[30] Mark Buchanan, *Hidden in Plain Sight: The Secret of More* (Nashville, Thomas Nelson, 2007), 180.

[31] John Eagan, *A Traveler Toward the Dawn: The Spiritual Journey of John Eagan* (Chicago: Loyola University Press, 1990), 150.

[32] Henri Nouwen, *Life of the Beloved: Spiritual Living in a Secular World* (New York: Crossroad, 1992), 21.

[33] Nouwen, *Life of the Beloved,* 26.

[34] Manning and Hancock, *Posers, Fakers and Wannabes,* 58–59.

[35] Thomas Merton, quoted by James Finley, *Merton's Place of Nowhere* (Notre Dame: Ave Maria Press, 1978), 53.

[36] Eldredge, *Walking with God,* 99–100.

[37] Neil Anderson, *The Bondage Breaker* (Eugene: Harvest House Publishers, 2006).

[38] Annie Dillard, *Teaching a Stone to Talk: Expeditions and Encounters* (New York: Harper & Row, 1982), 43.

[39] Jeffrey D. Imbach, *The Recovery of Love: Christian Mysticism and the Addictive Society* (New York: Crossroad, 1992), 62–63.

[40] Buchanan, *Spiritual Rhythms,* 125.

[41] Manning and Hancock, *Posers, Fakers and Wannabes,* 65.

[42] Buchanan, *Hidden in Plain Sight,* 103.

[43] Eldredge, *Walking with God,* 13–14.

[44] Jerry Bridges, *The Pursuit of Holiness* (Colorado Springs: NavPress, 2006).

[45] Manning and Hancock, *Posers, Fakers and Wannabes,* 61.

[46] Manning, *Abba's Child,* 52–53.

[47] Richard J. Foster, *Celebration of Discipline: The Path to Spiritual Growth* (New York: HarperCollins, 1988); Dallas Willard, *The Spirit of the Disciplines: How God Changes Lives* (New York: HarperCollins, 1988); John Ortberg, *The Life You've Always Wanted: Spiritual Disciplines for Ordinary People* (Grand Rapids: Zondervan, 2002).

[48] Mark Buchanan, *The Rest of God: Restoring Your Soul by Restoring Sabbath* (Nashville: Thomas Nelson, 2006), 129.

[49] Curtis and Eldredge, *Sacred Romance,* 5.

[50] John Eldredge, *Dare to Desire: An Invitation to Fulfill your Deepest Dreams* (Nashville: J. Countryman, 2002), chapter 3, e-book edition.

[51] John Eldredge, *Desire: The Journey We Must Take to Find the Life God Offers* (Nashville: Thomas Nelson, 2000), viii–ix.

[52] Manning and Hancock, *Posers, Fakers and Wannabes,* 147.

[53] Eldredge, *Desire,* 41.

[54] Eldredge, *Desire,* 41.

[55] Curtis and Eldredge, *Sacred Romance,* 200–201.

[56] Martin Luther, Letter 99, Paragraph 13 in *Dr. Martin Luther's Saemmtlliche Schriften*, Vol. 15, ed. Dr. Johann George Walch, trans. Erika Bullmann Flores (St. Louis: Concordia, date unknown), 2585–2590.

[57] Martin Luther, *Faith Alone: A Daily Devotional, an Updated Edition in Today's Language*, ed. James C. Calvin (Grand Rapids: Zondervan, 2005), February 21 entry.

[58] Luther, *Faith Alone*, April 18 entry.

[59] Buchanan, *Hidden in Plain Sight*, 45.

[60] John Eldredge, *Waking the Dead* (Nashville: Thomas Nelson, 2006), 95.

[61] *Thought He Would* (Nashville: Thomas Nelson, 2010), 50.

[62] Buchanan, *Spiritual Rhythms*, 128–129.

[63] Buchanan, *Spiritual Rhythms*, 128.

[64] Manning, *Abba's Child*, 59.

[65] Manning, *Abba's Child*, 160.

[66] Manning, *Abba's Child*, 159.

[67] Ortberg, *The Me I Want to Be*, 21.

[68] Henri J. M. Nouwen, *Can you Drink this Cup?* (Notre Dame: Ave Maria Press, 1996), 89.

Castle Quay Books
WWW.CASTLEQUAYBOOKS.COM

Other Award Winning Castle Quay titles include:

Bent Hope (Tim Huff)

The Beautiful Disappointment (Colin McCartney)

The Cardboard Shack Beneath the Bridge (Tim Huff)

Certainty (Grant Richison) - **NEW!**

Dancing with Dynamite (Tim Huff) - **NEW!** 2011 Book of the Year Award!

Deciding to Know God in a Deeper Way (Sam Tita) - **NEW!**

The Defilers (Deborah Gyapong)

Father to the Fatherless (Paul Boge)

Find a Broken Wall (Brian Stiller) - **NEW!**

Hope for the Hopeless (Paul Boge) - **NEW!**

I Sat Where They Sat (Arnold Bowler)

Jesus and Caesar (Brian Stiller)

Keep On Standing (Darlene Polachic)

The Kingdom Promise (Gary Gradley & Phil Kershaw)

The Leadership Edge (Elaine Stewart-Rhude)

Leaving a Legacy (David C. Bentall) - **NEW!**

Making Your Dreams Your Destiny (Judy Rushfeldt)

Mentoring Wisdom (Dr. Carson Pue) - **NEW!**

Mere Christian (Michael Coren)

Mormon Crisis (James Beverley)

One Smooth Stone (Marcia Lee Laycock)

Our Father: the Prodigal Son Returns (Pastor Bruce Smith & Phil Kershaw)

Predators Live Among Us: Protect Your Family from Child Sex Abuse
(Diane Roblin-Lee) - **NEW!**

Red Letter Revolution (Colin McCartney)

Reflections (Cal Bombay) - **NEW!**

Seven Angels for Seven Days (Angelina Fast-Vlaar)

Stop Preaching and Start Communicating (Tony Gentilucci) - **NEW!**

Through Fire & Sea (Marilyn Meyers)

To My Family (Diane Roblin-Lee)

Vision that Works (David Collins)

Walking Towards Hope (Paul Boge)

What Happens When I Die (Brian Stiller) - **NEW!**

The Way They Should Go (Kirsten Femson)

You Never Know What You Have Till You Give It Away (Brian Stiller)

For a full list of all Castle Quay and BayRidge book titles visit
www.castlequaybooks.com